I0504979

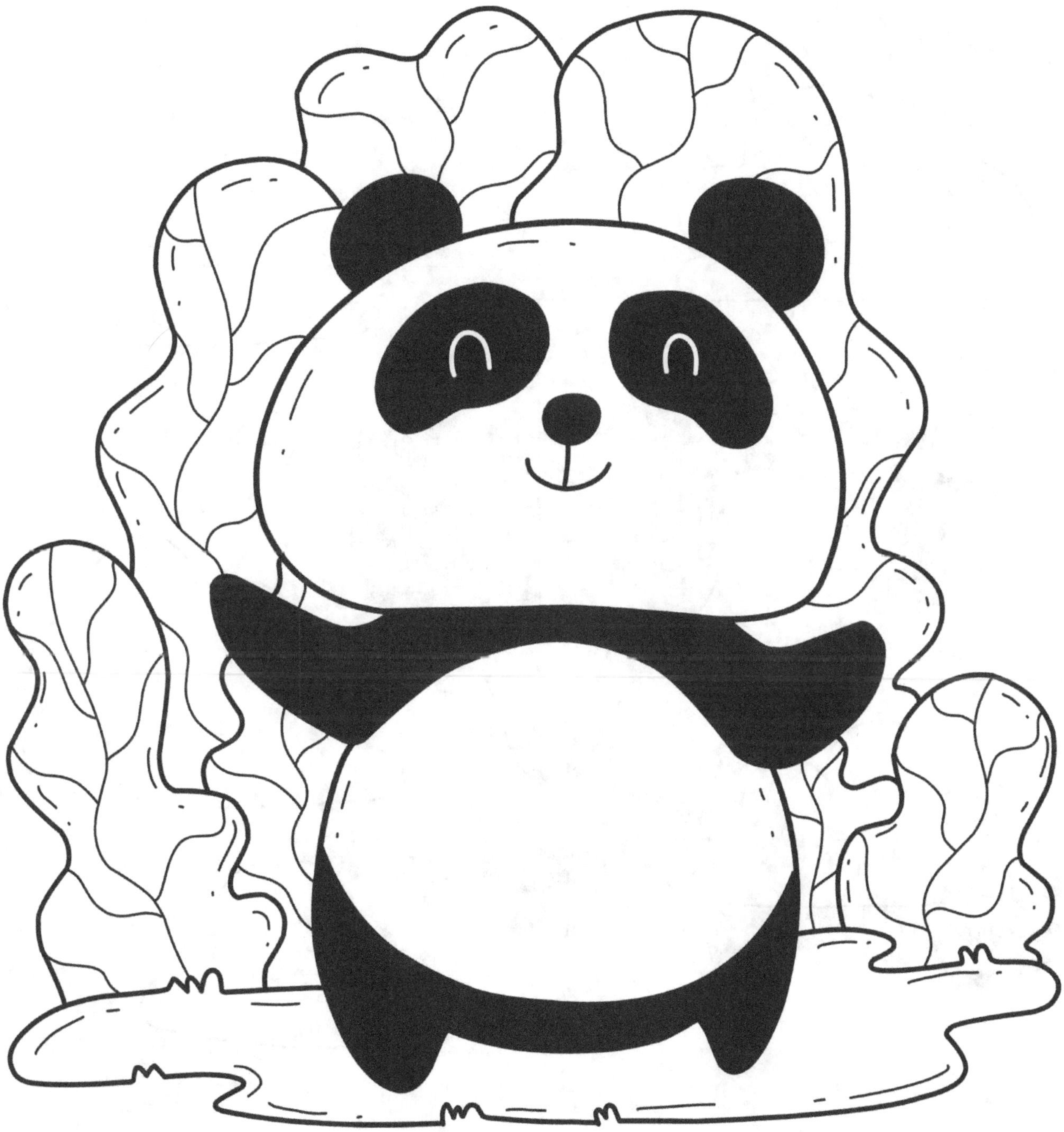

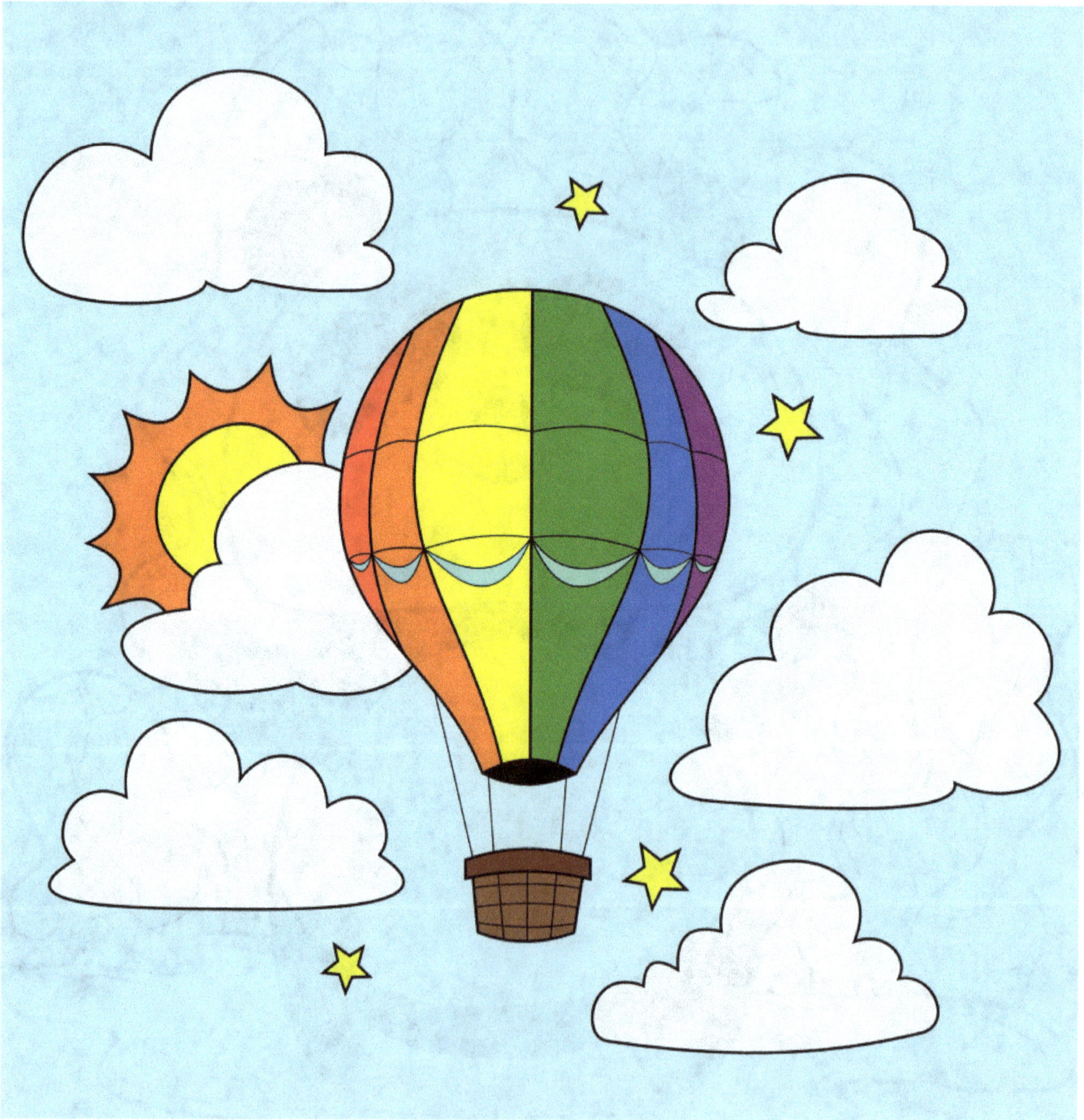

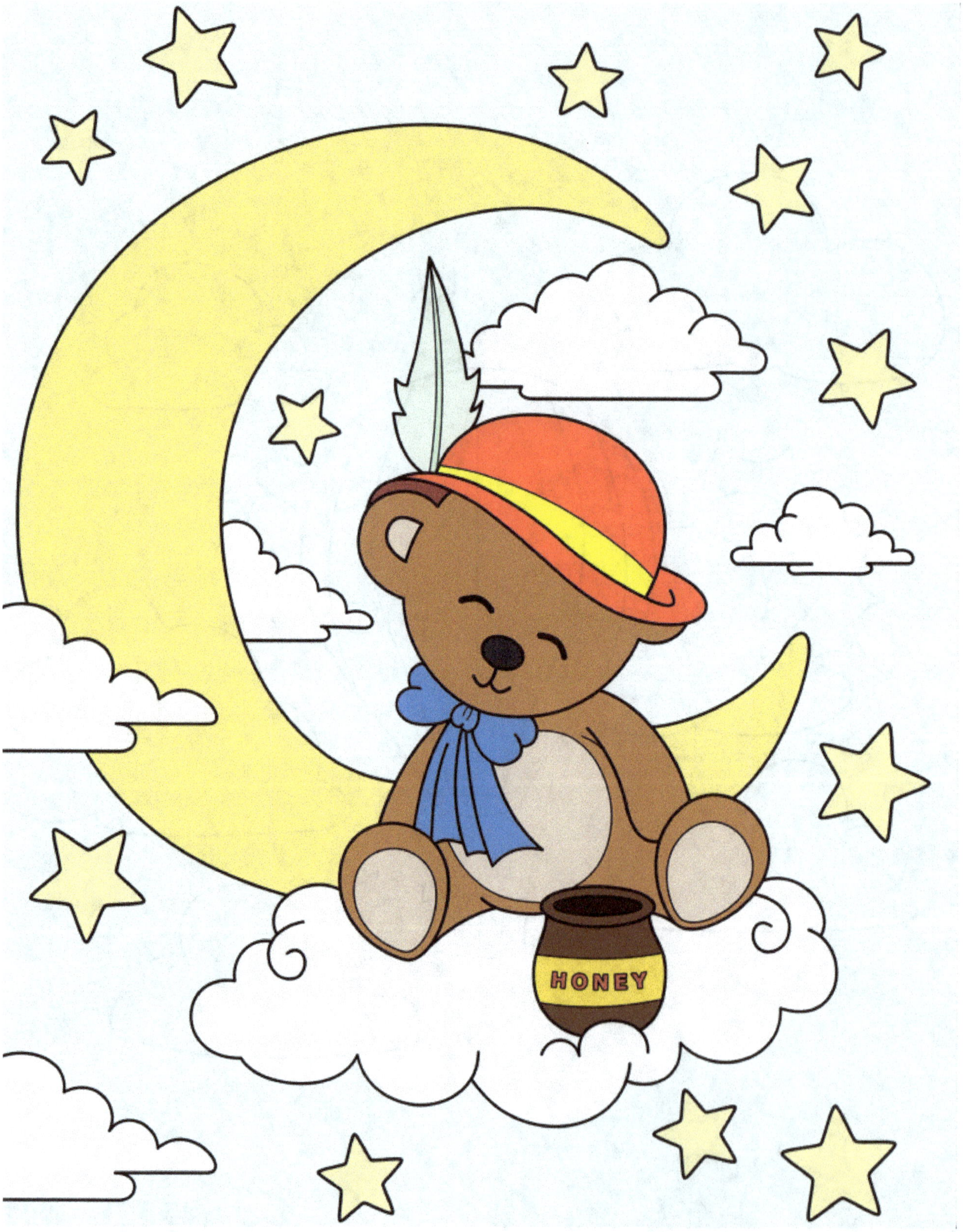
HONEY

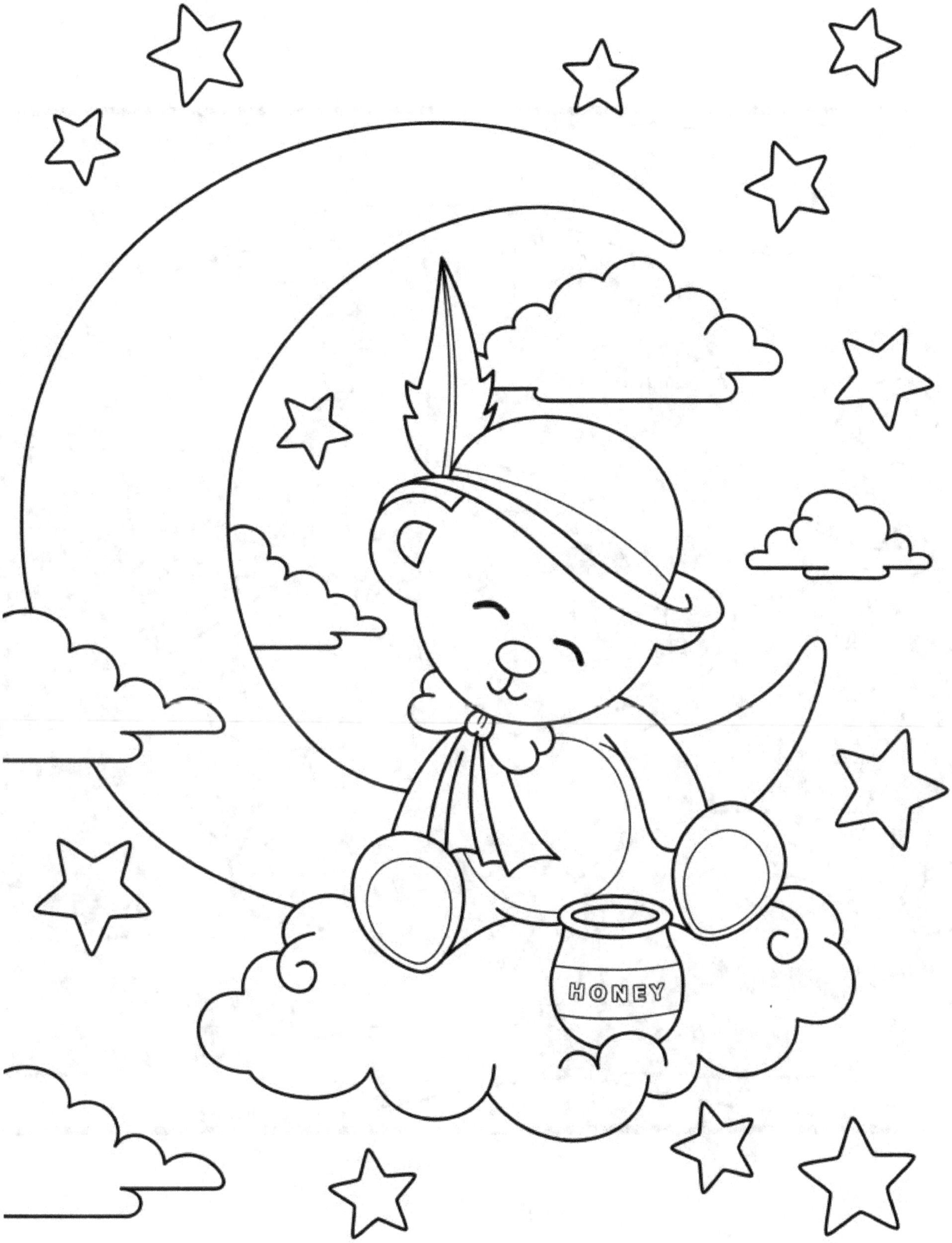
HONEY

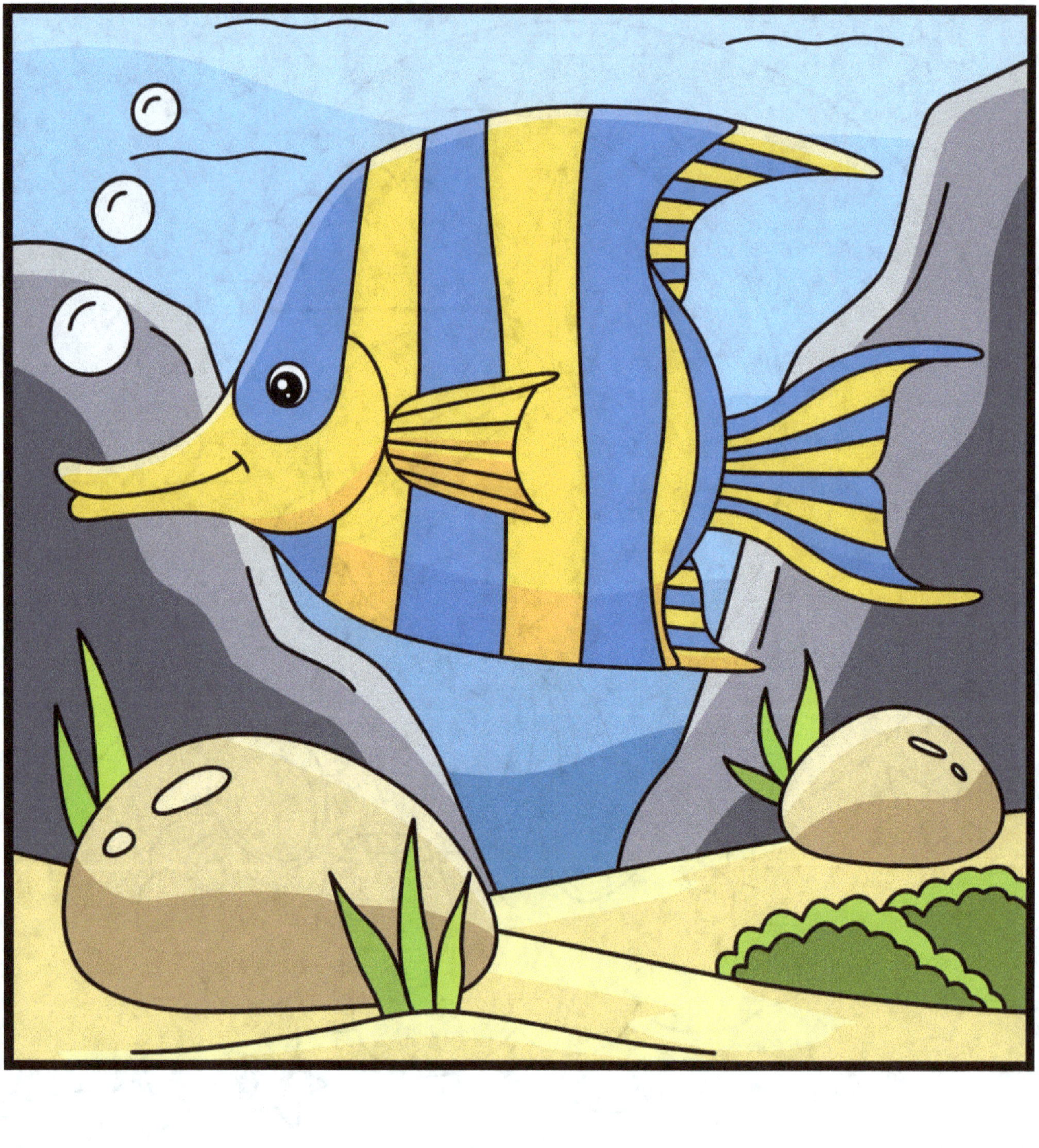

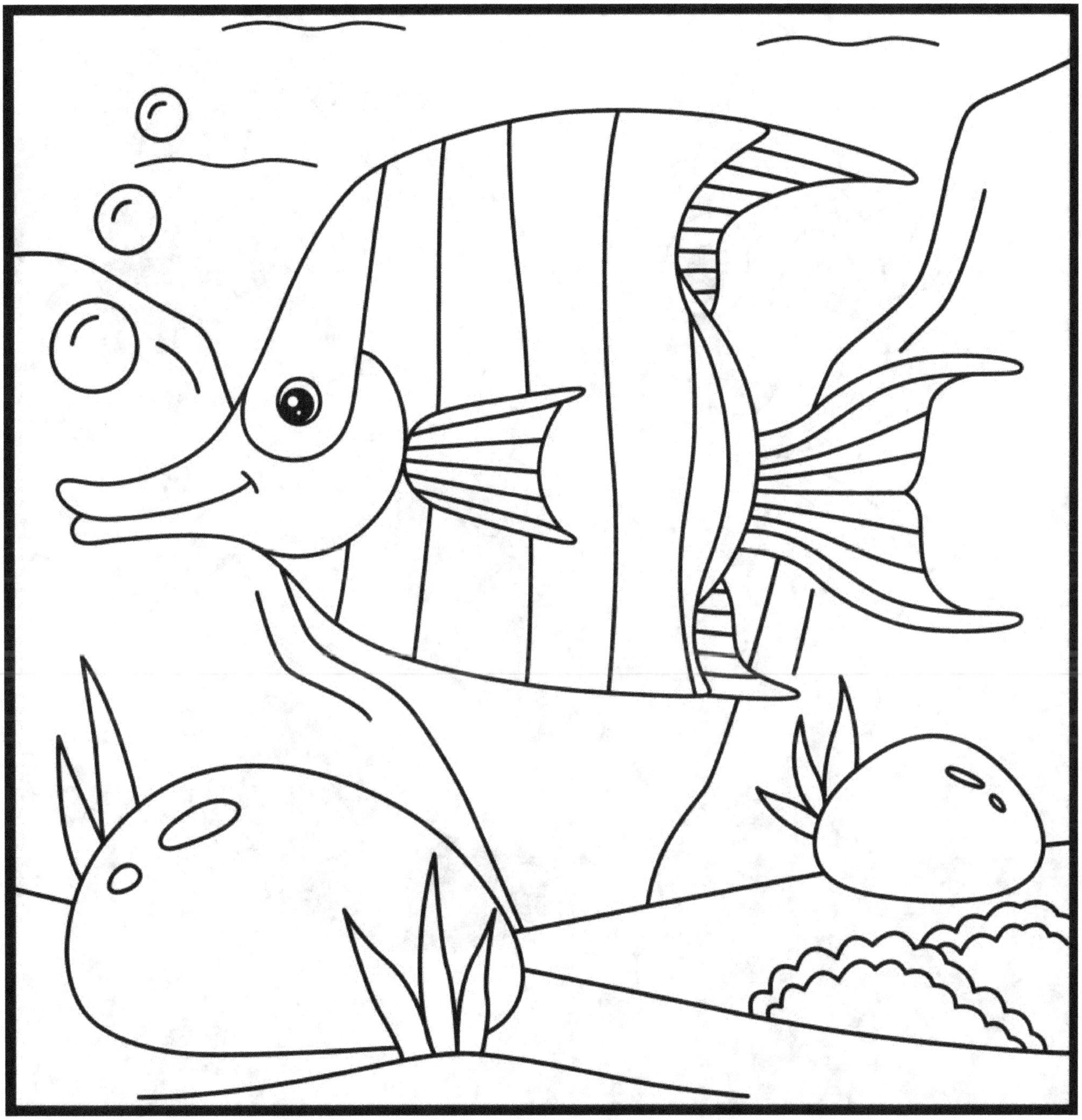

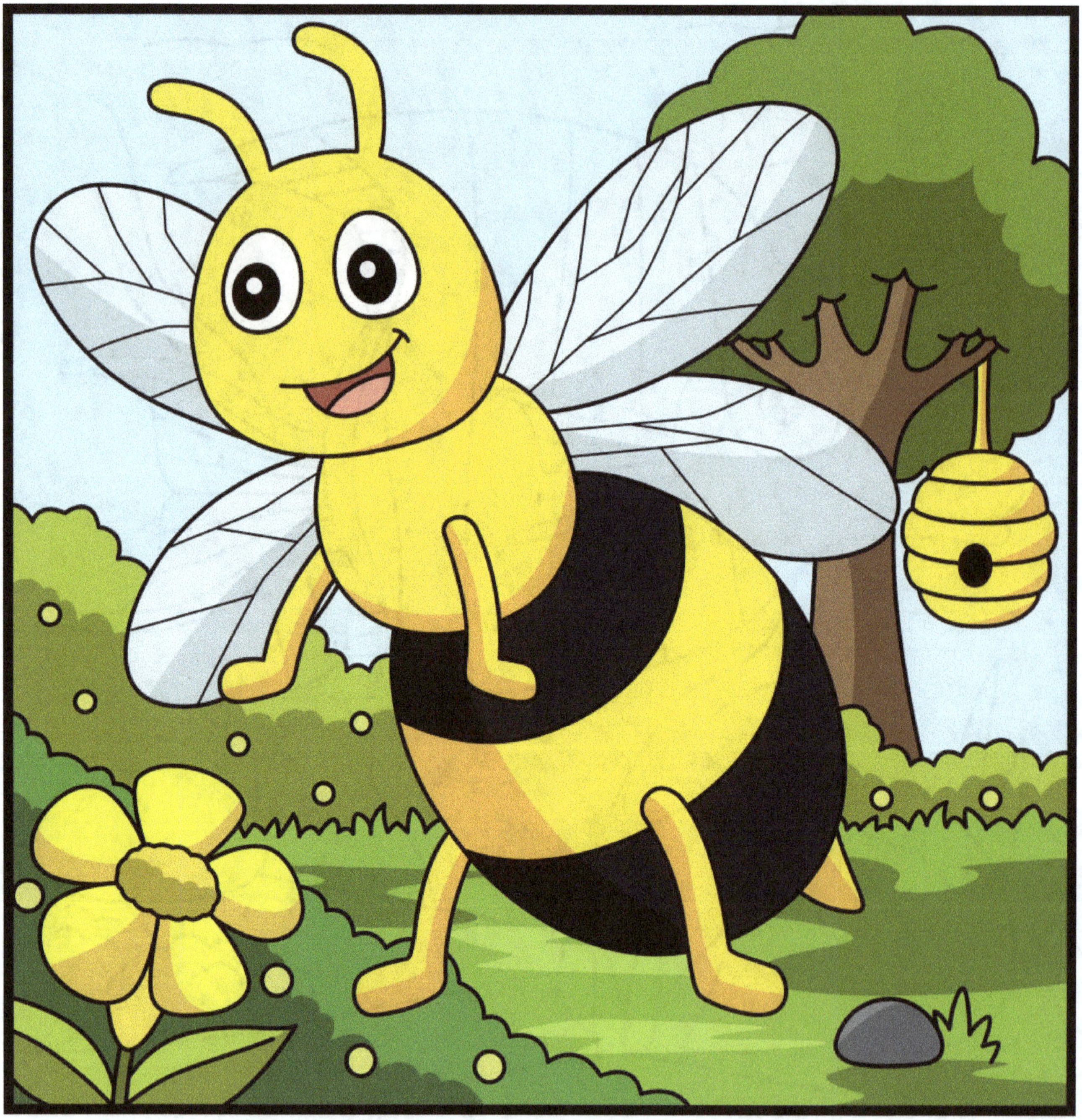

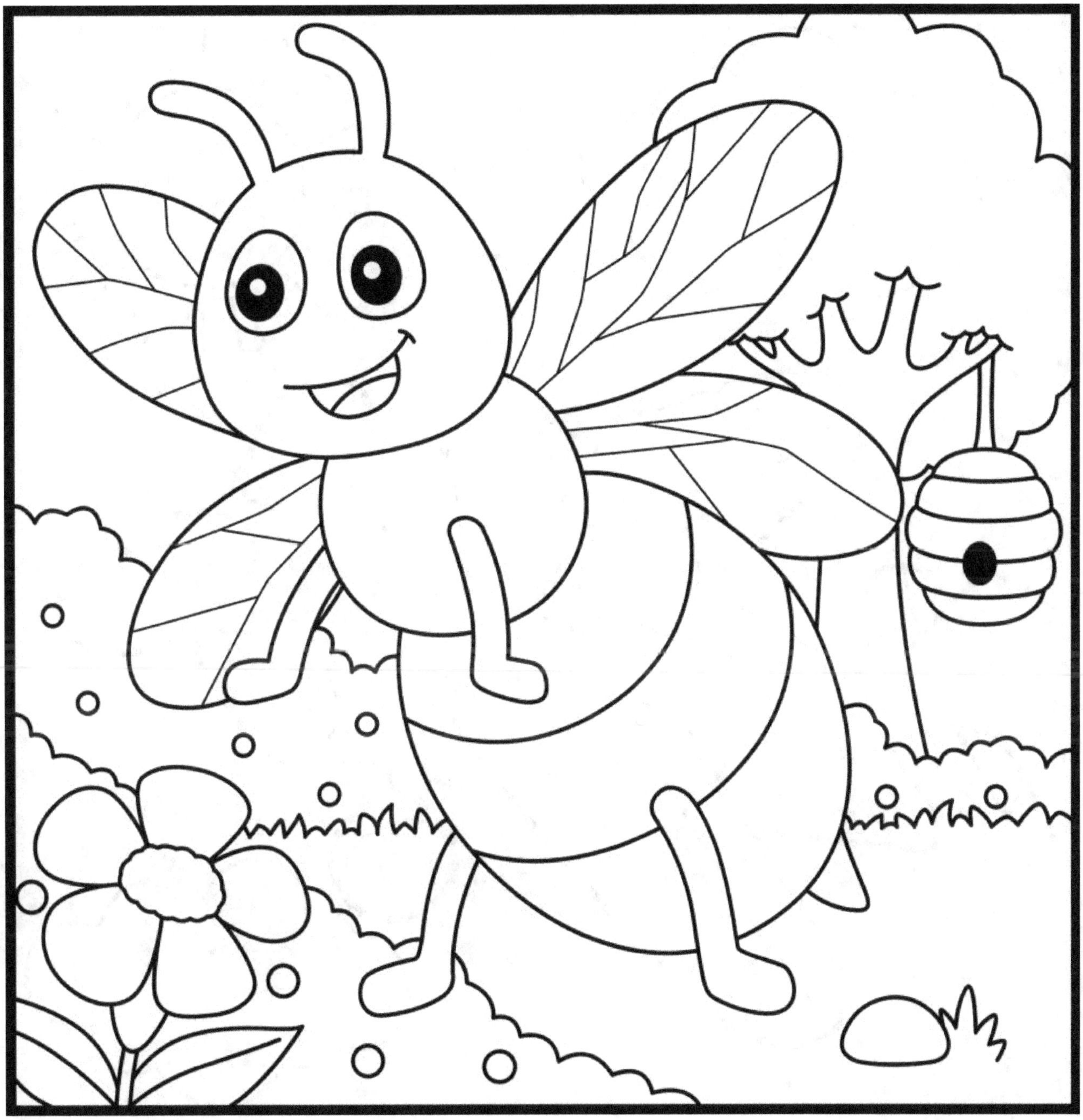

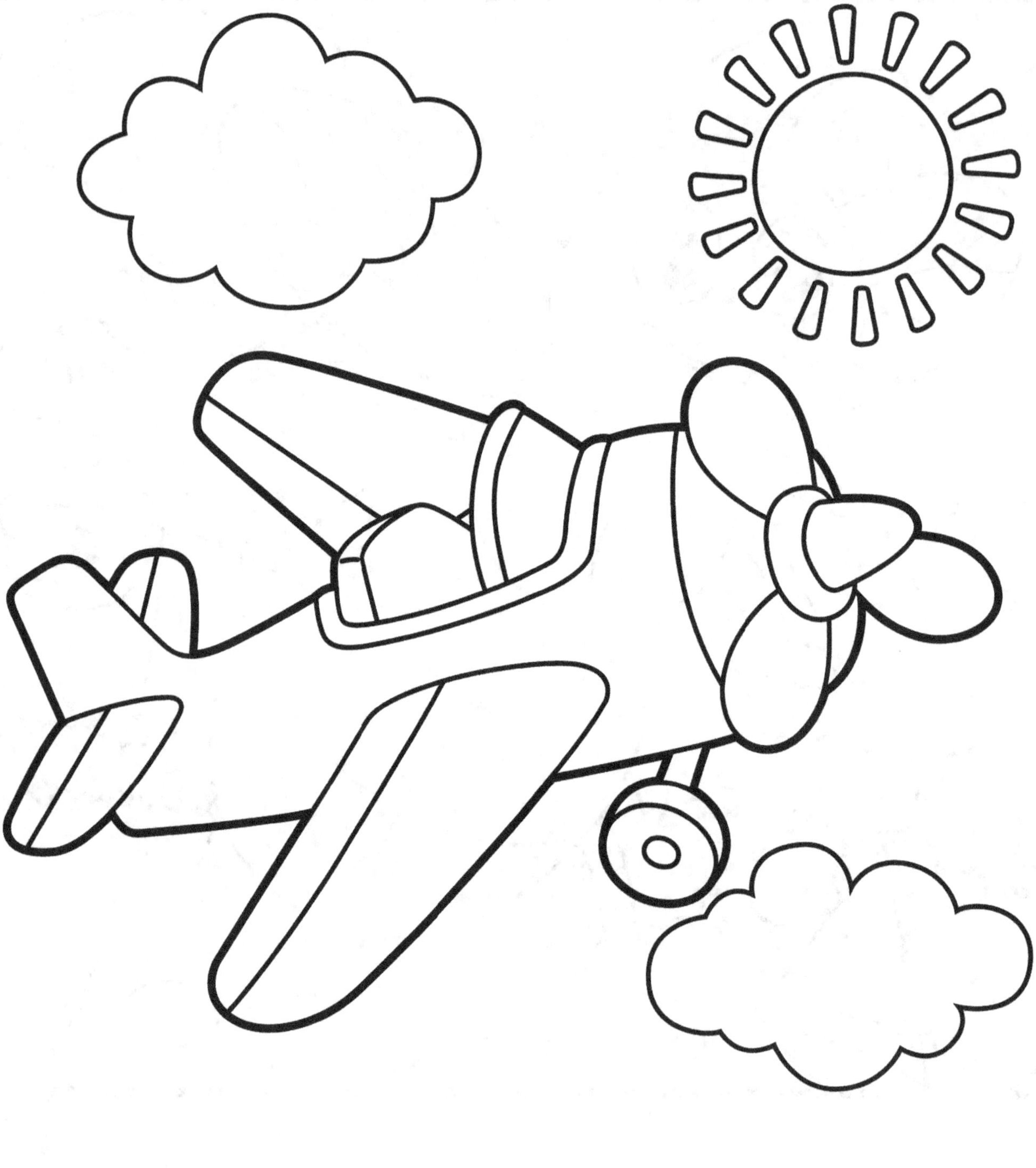

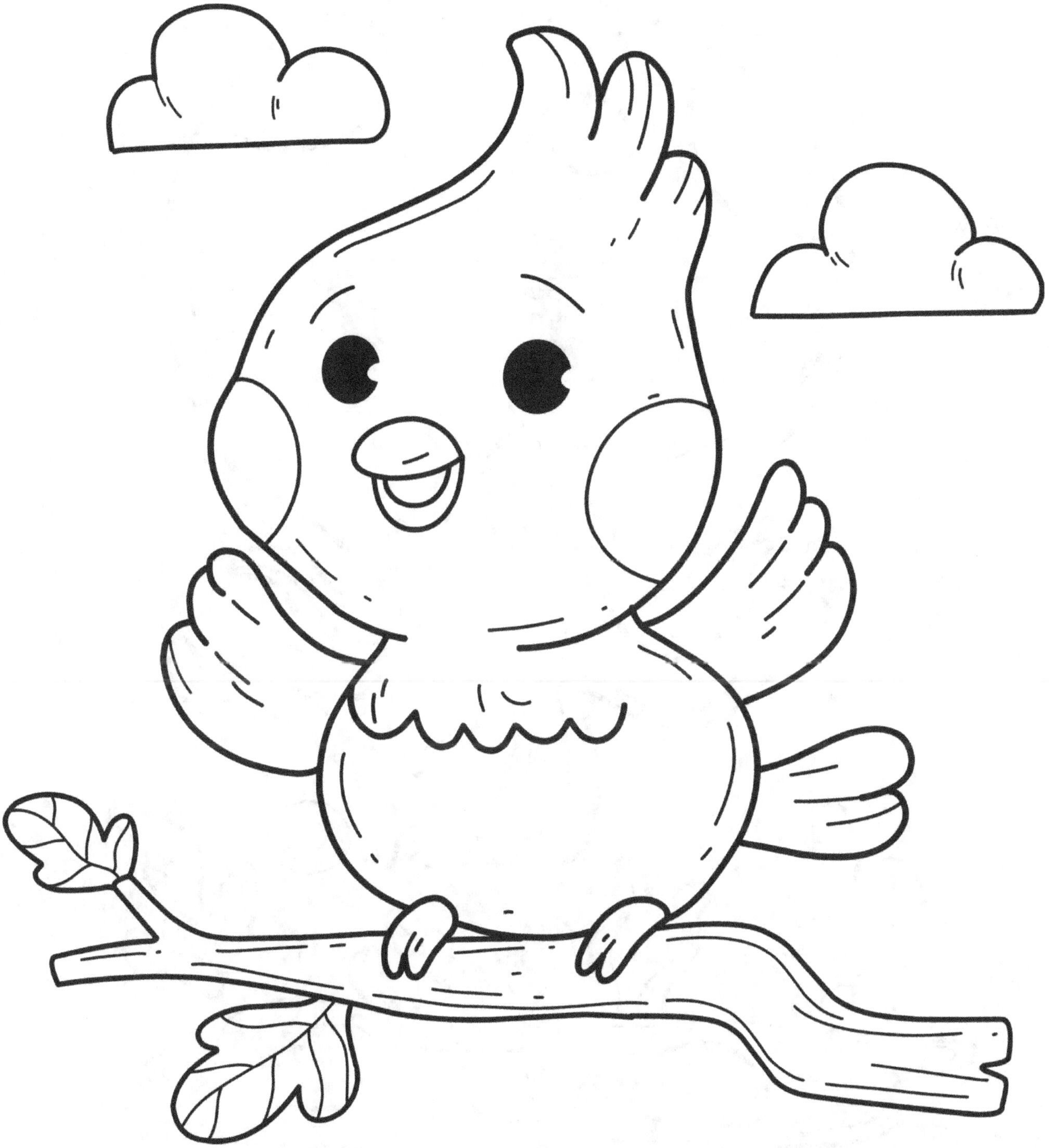

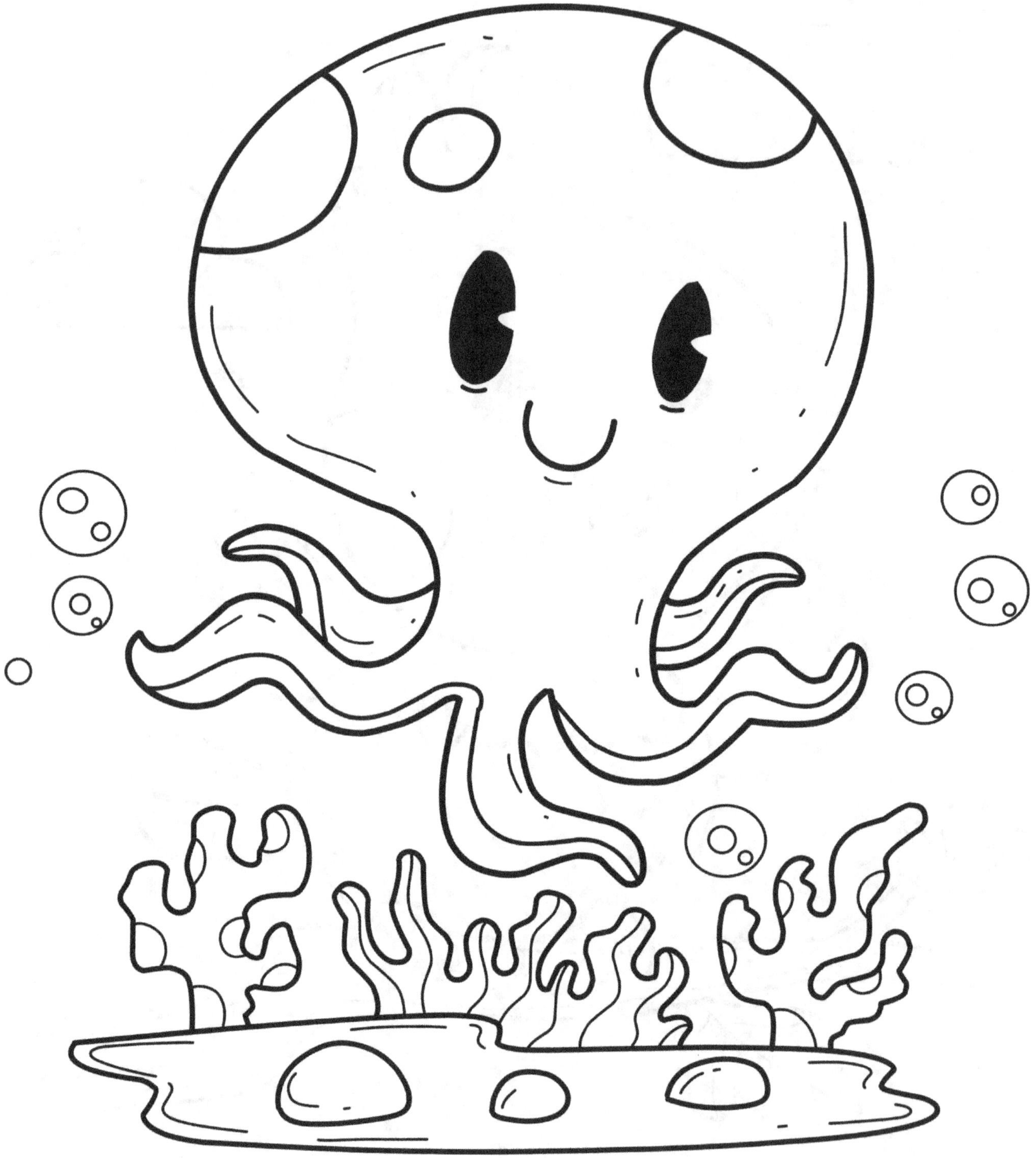

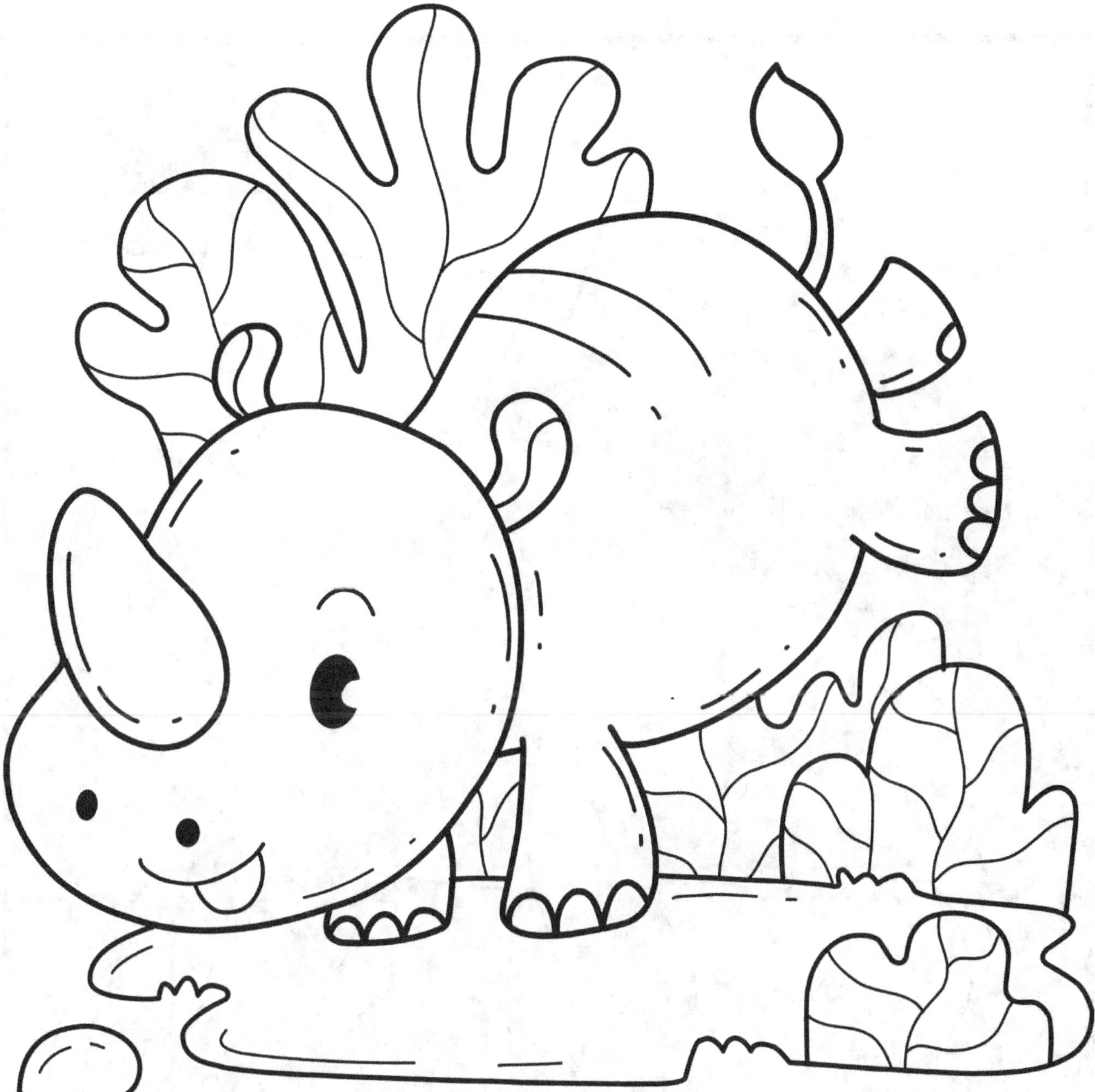

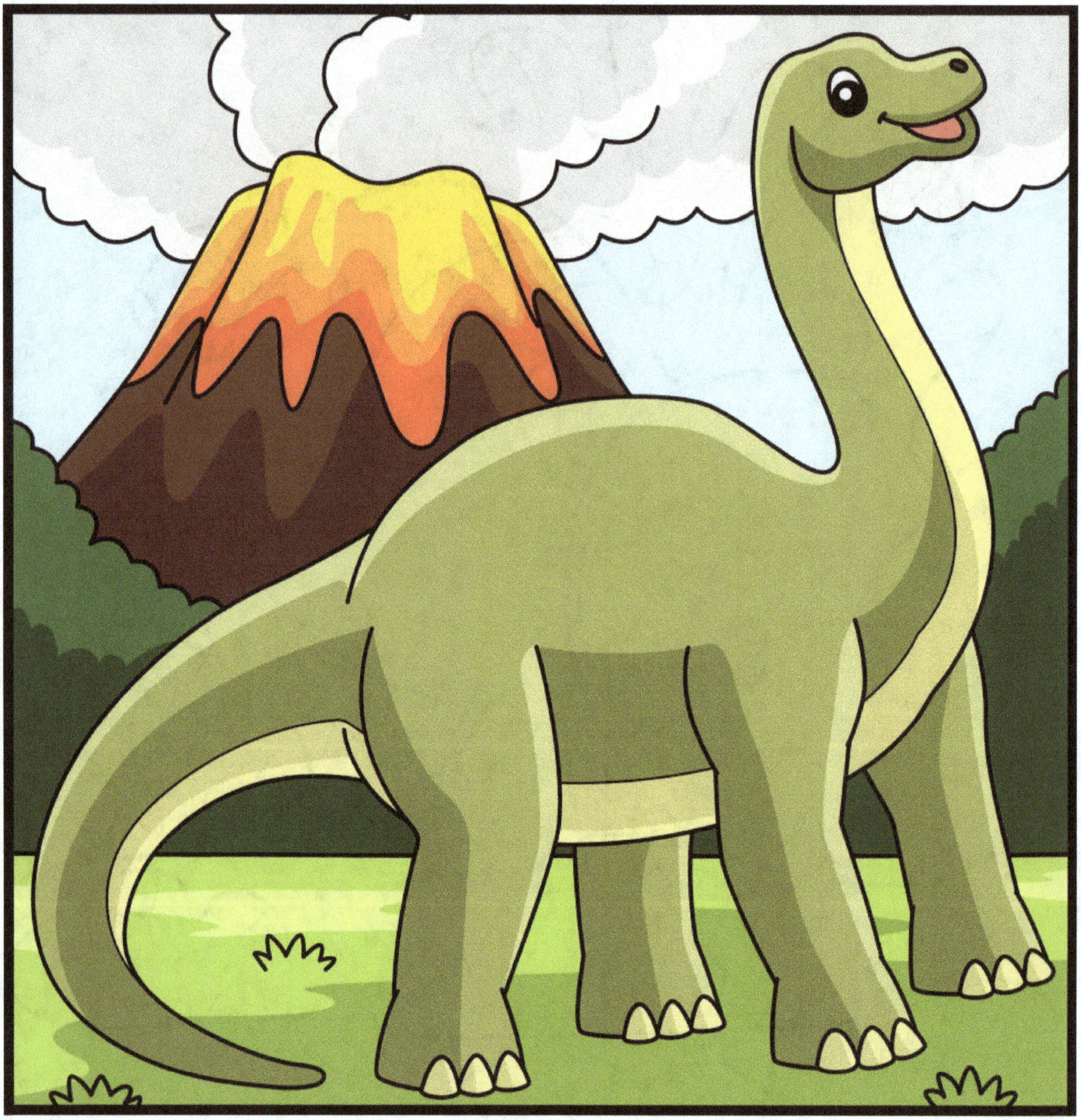

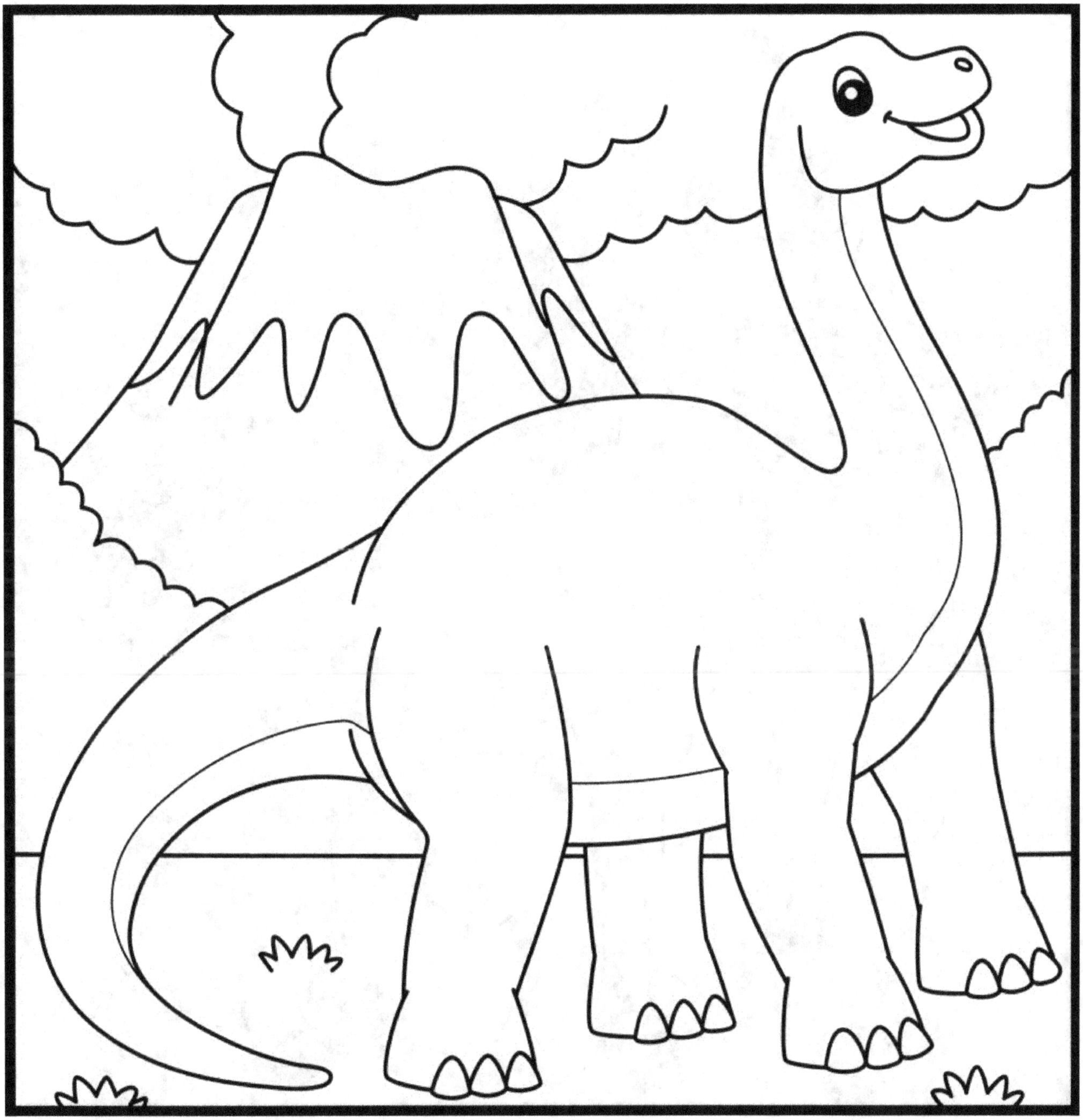

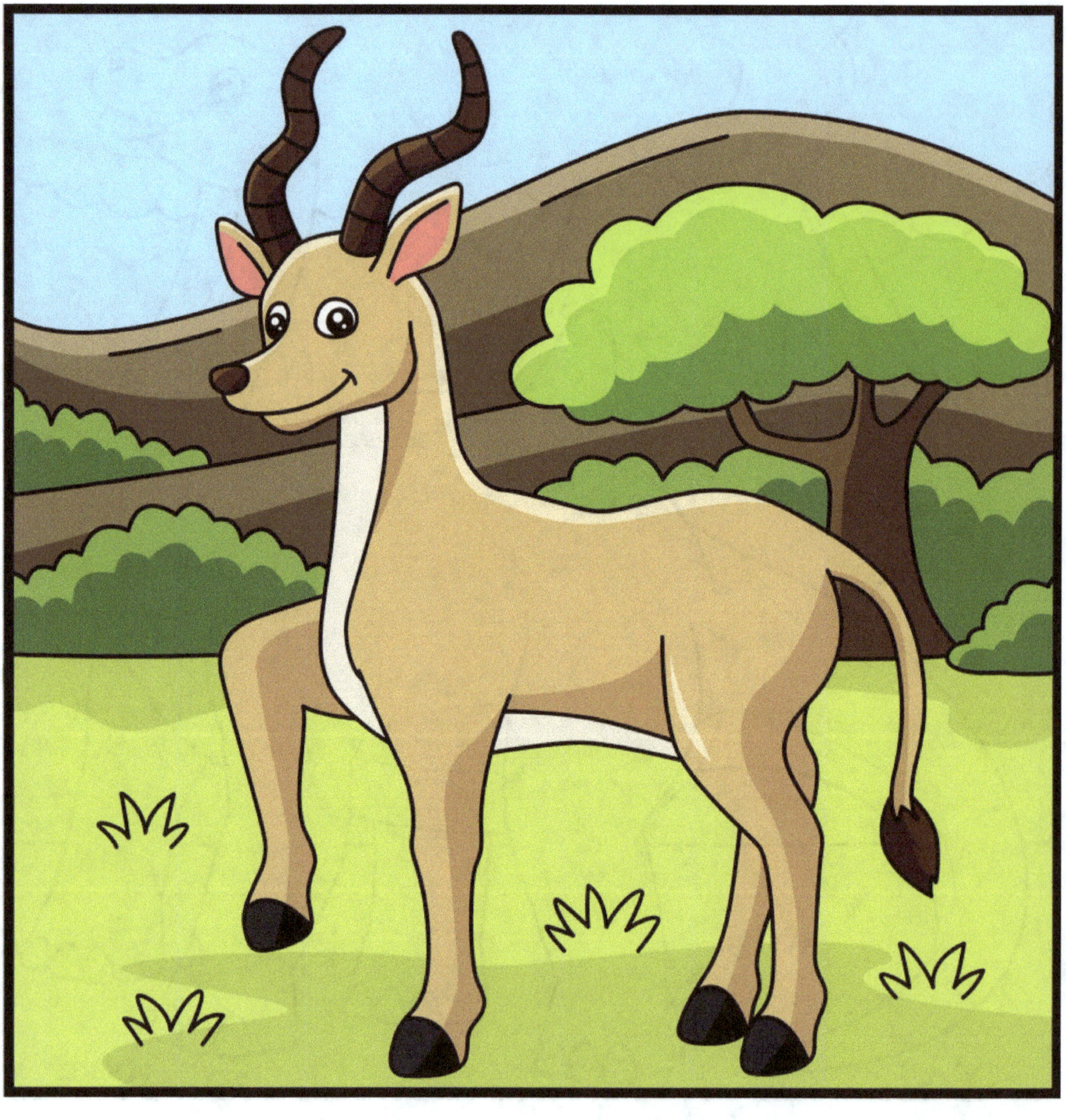

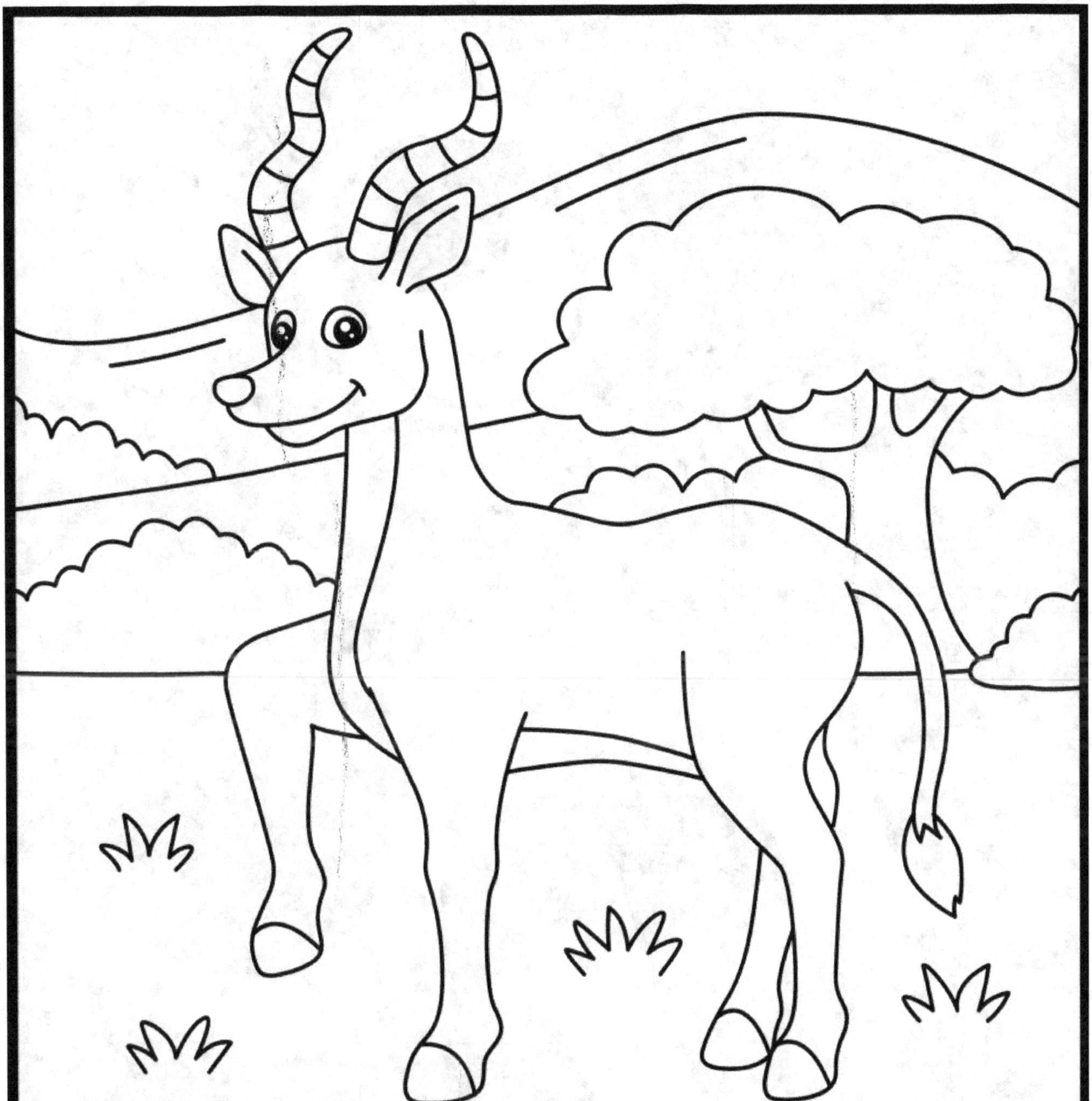

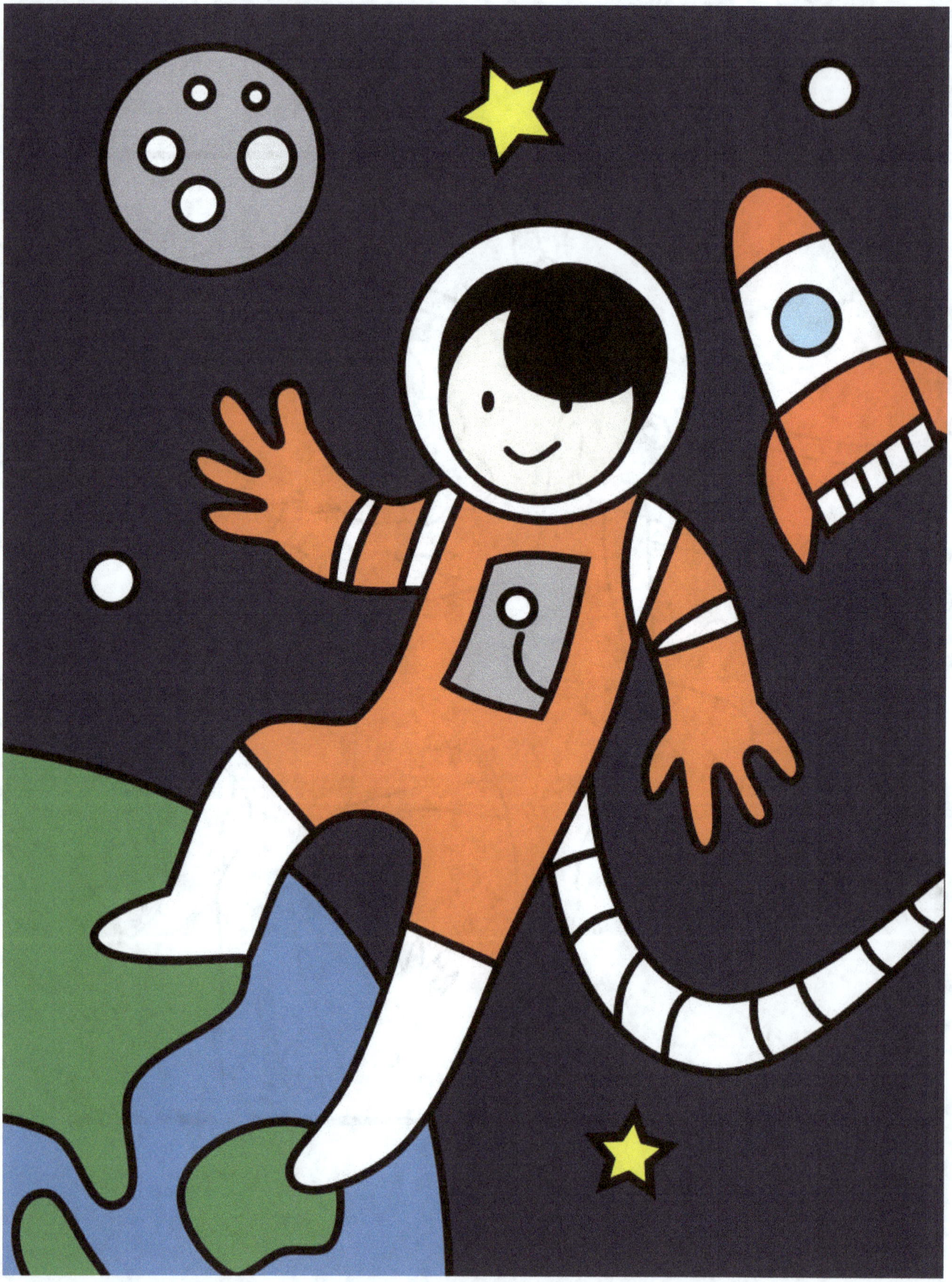

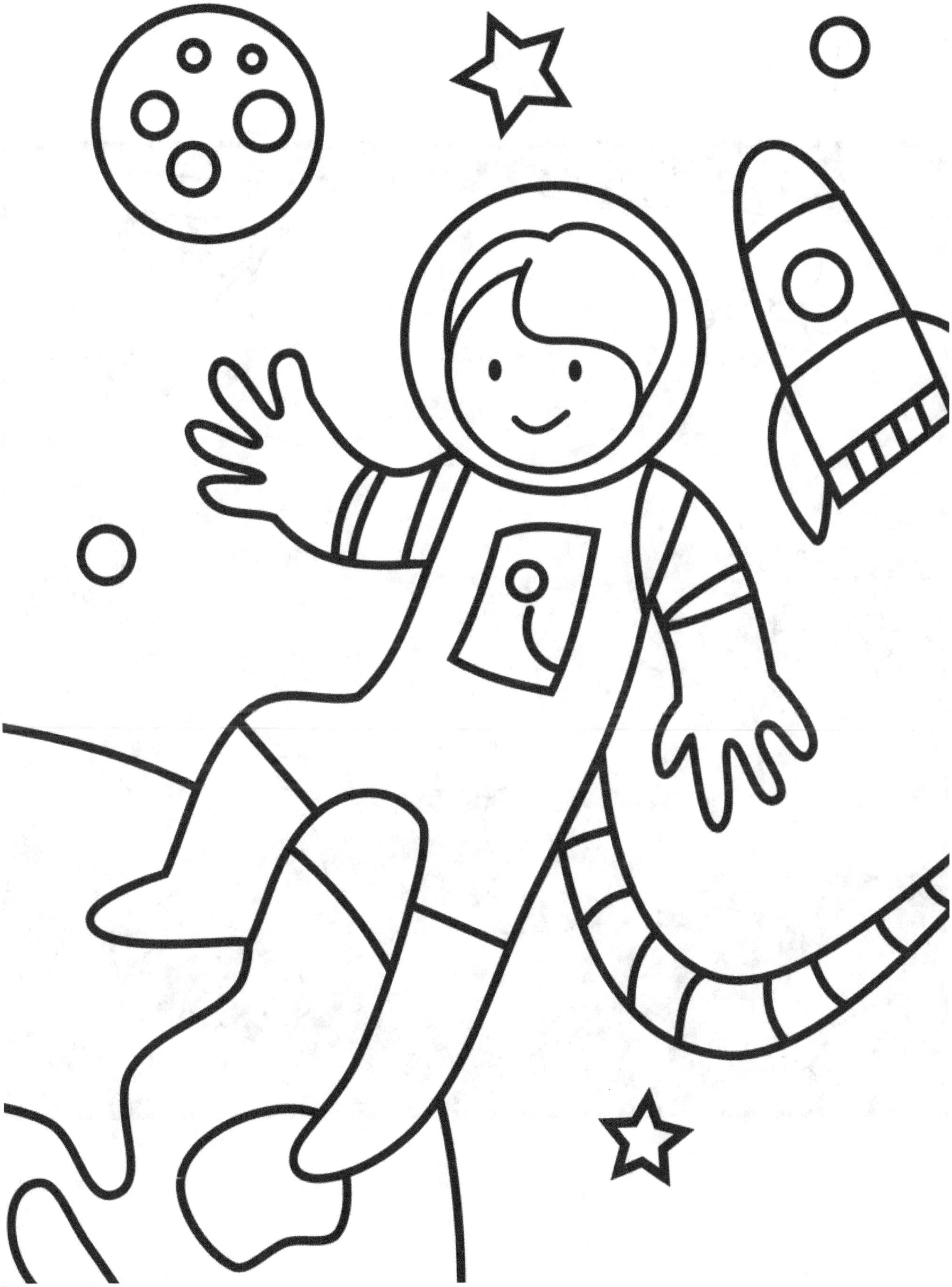

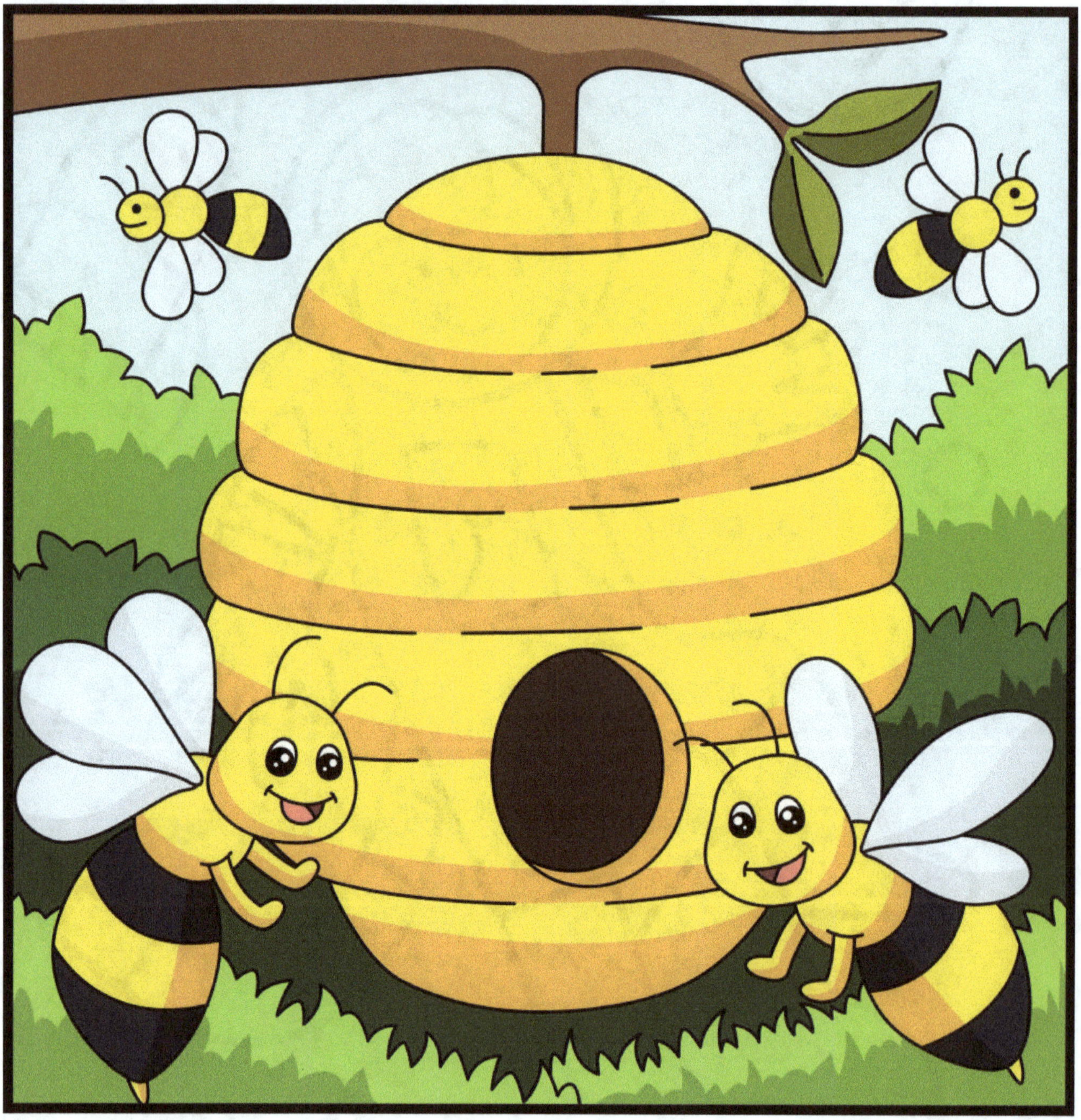

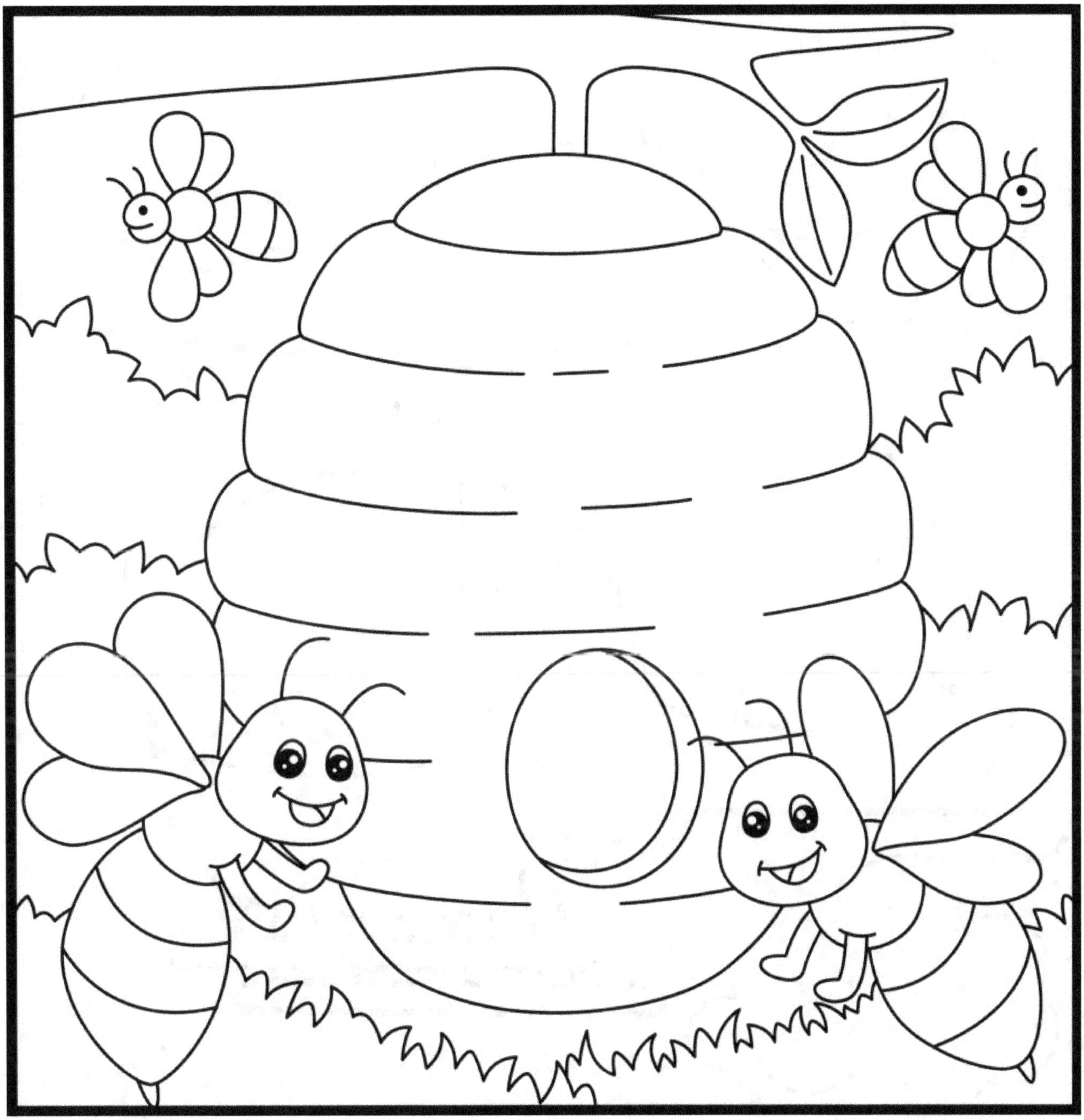

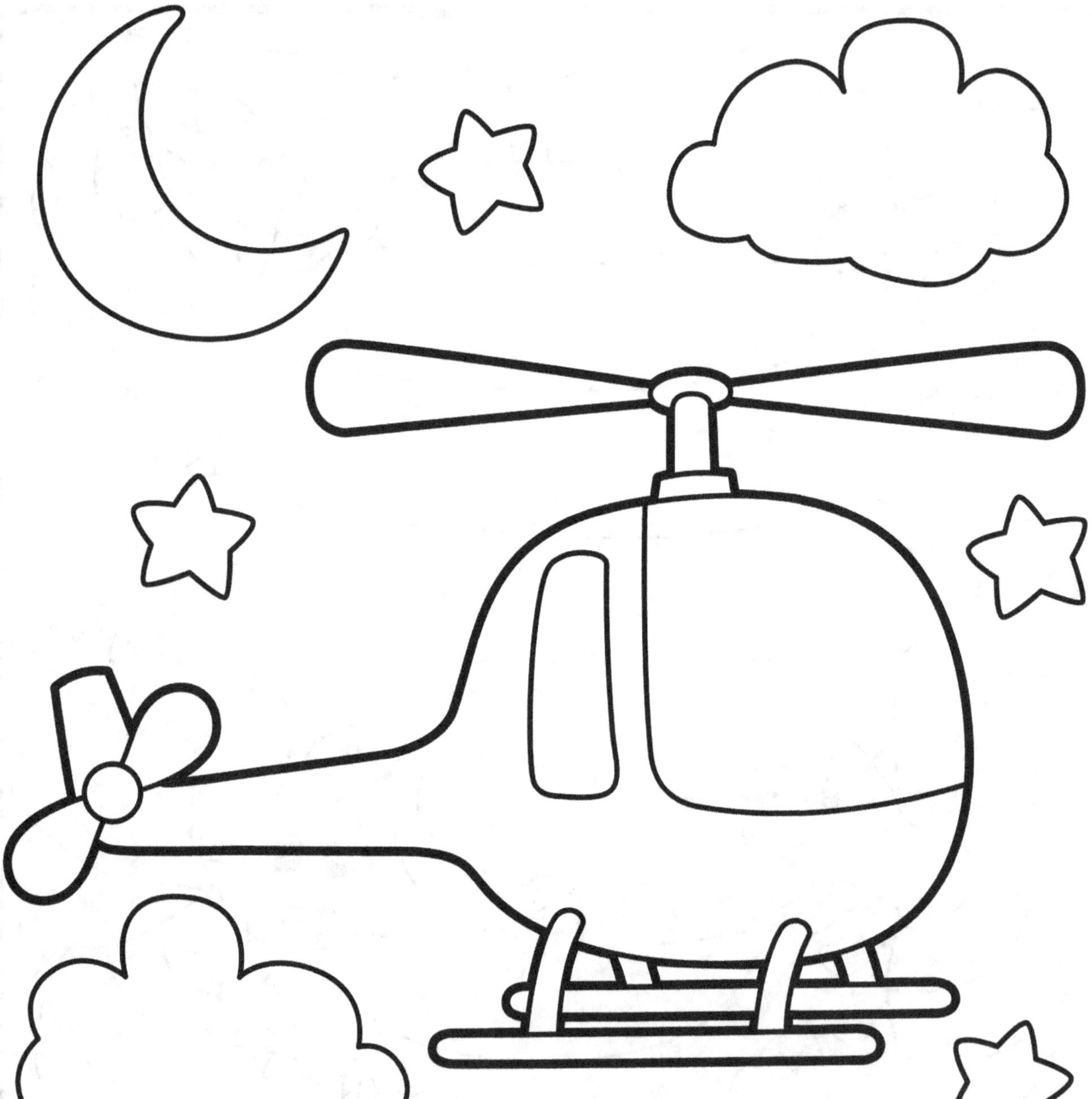

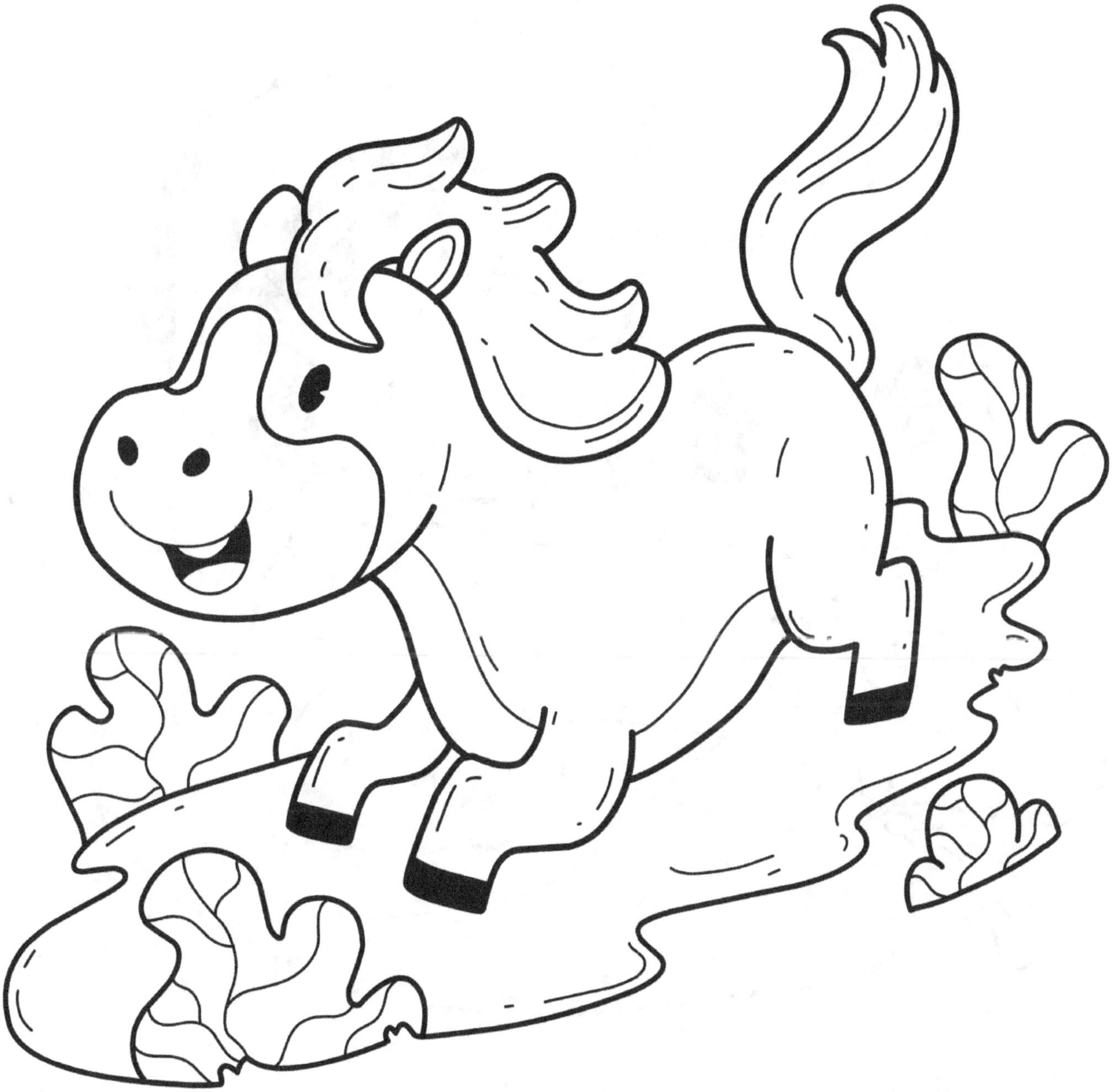

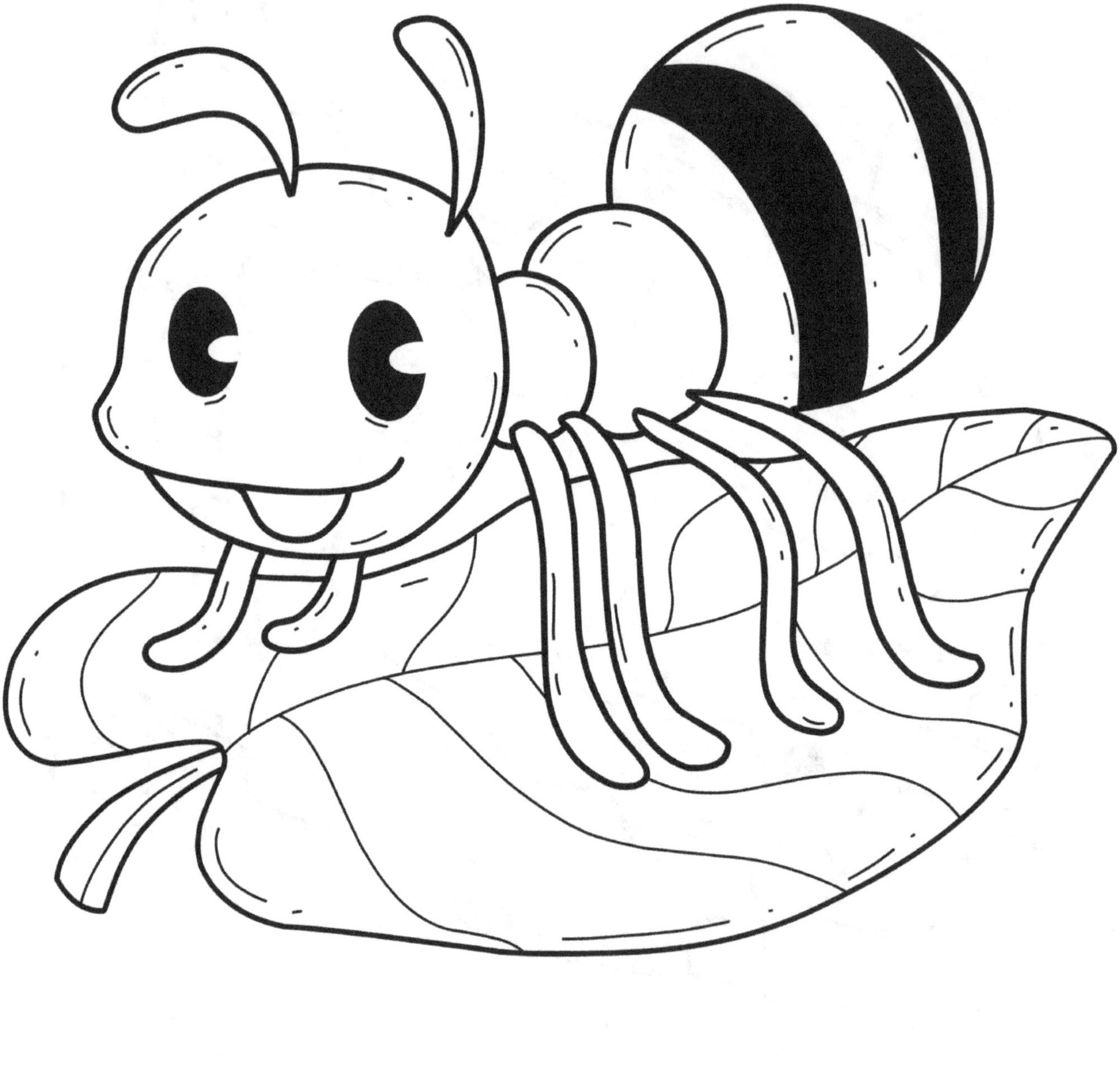

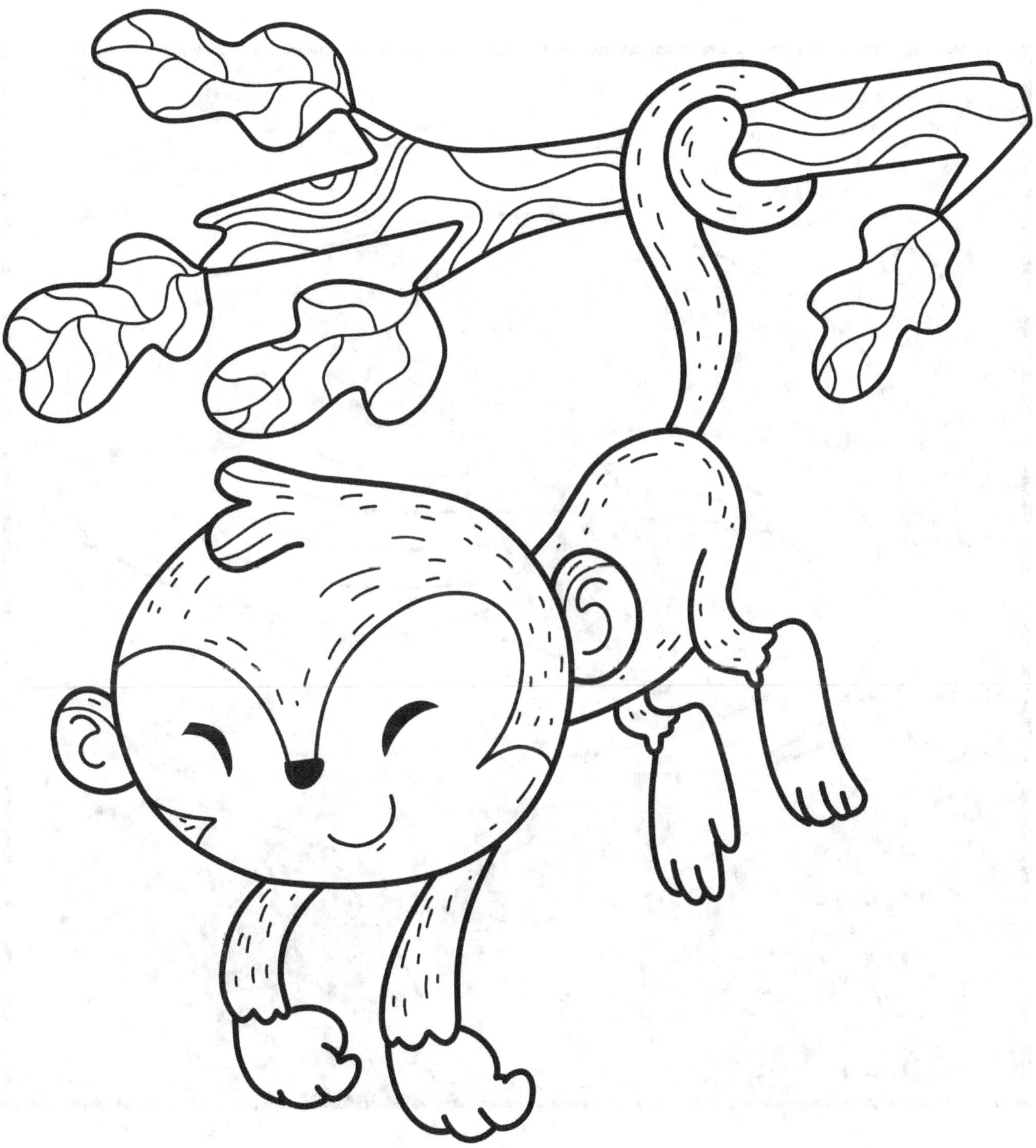

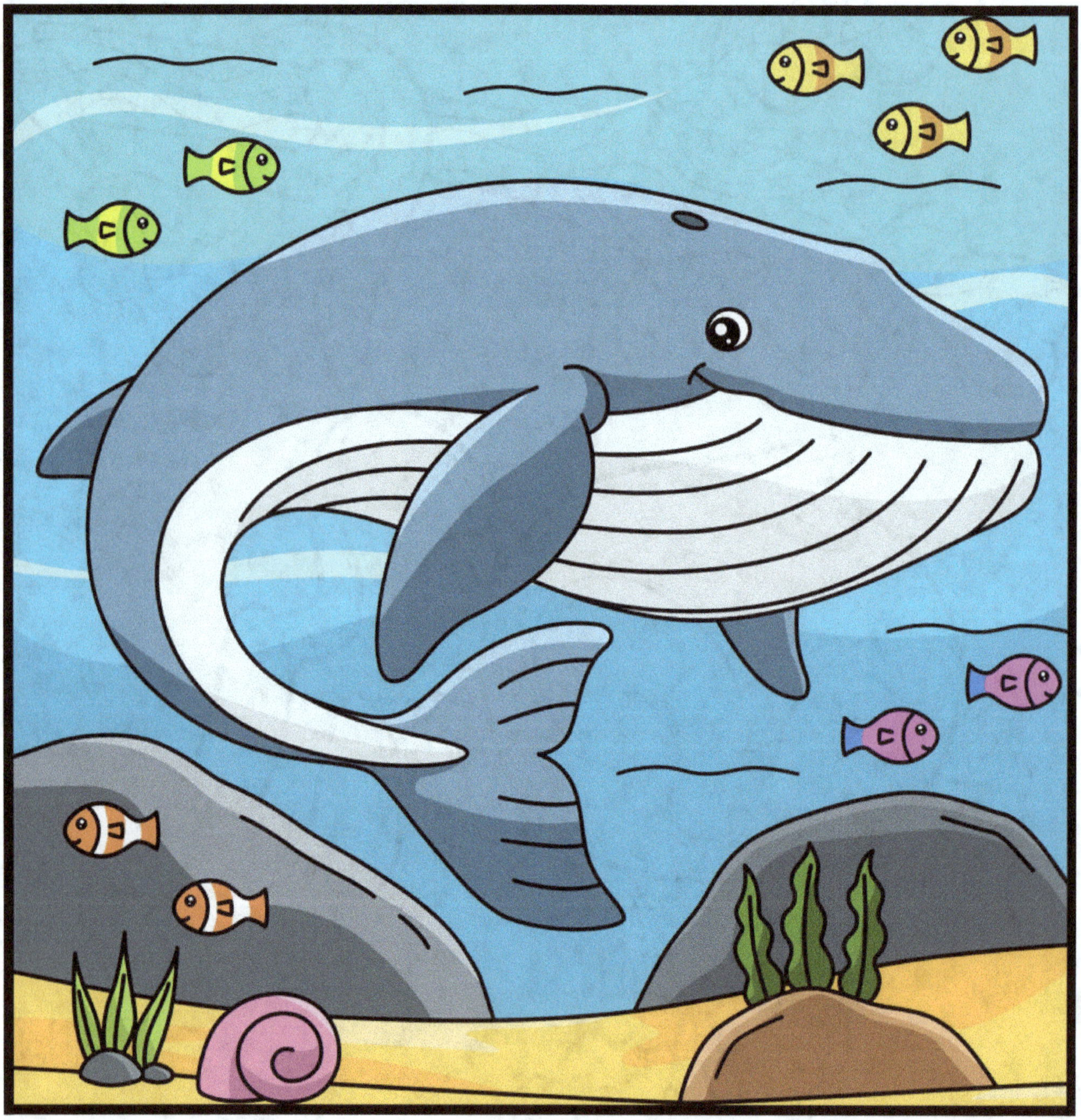

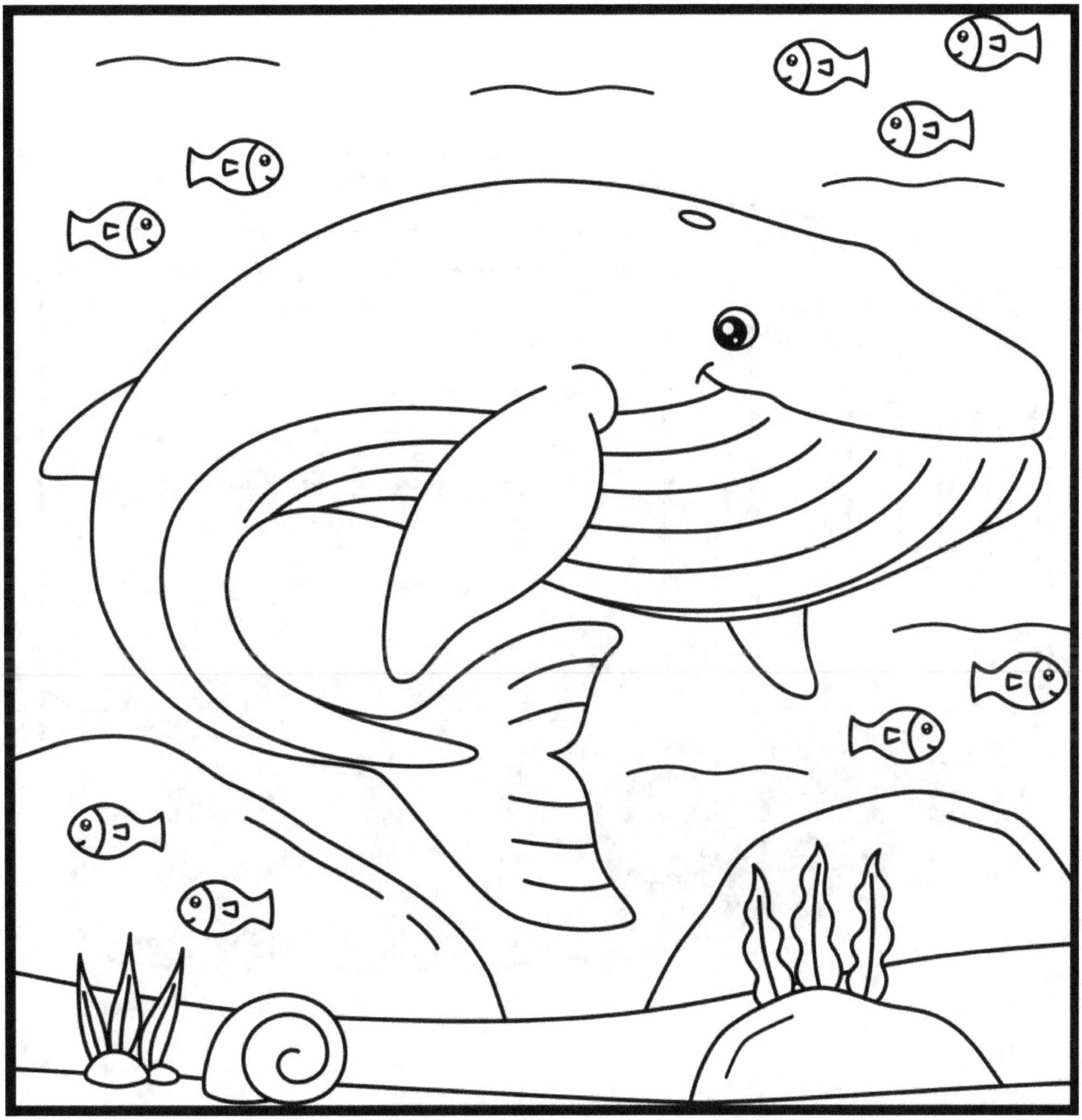

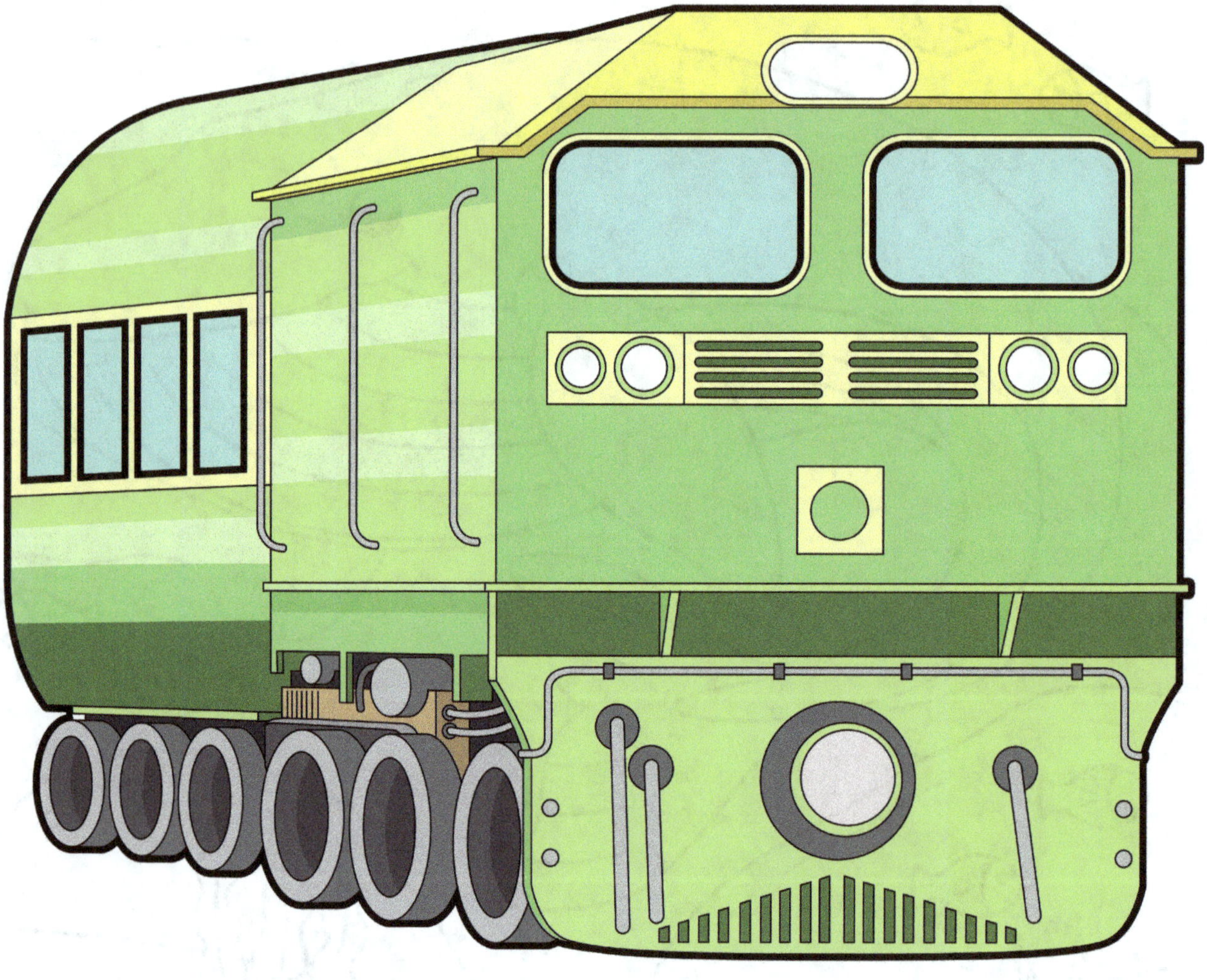

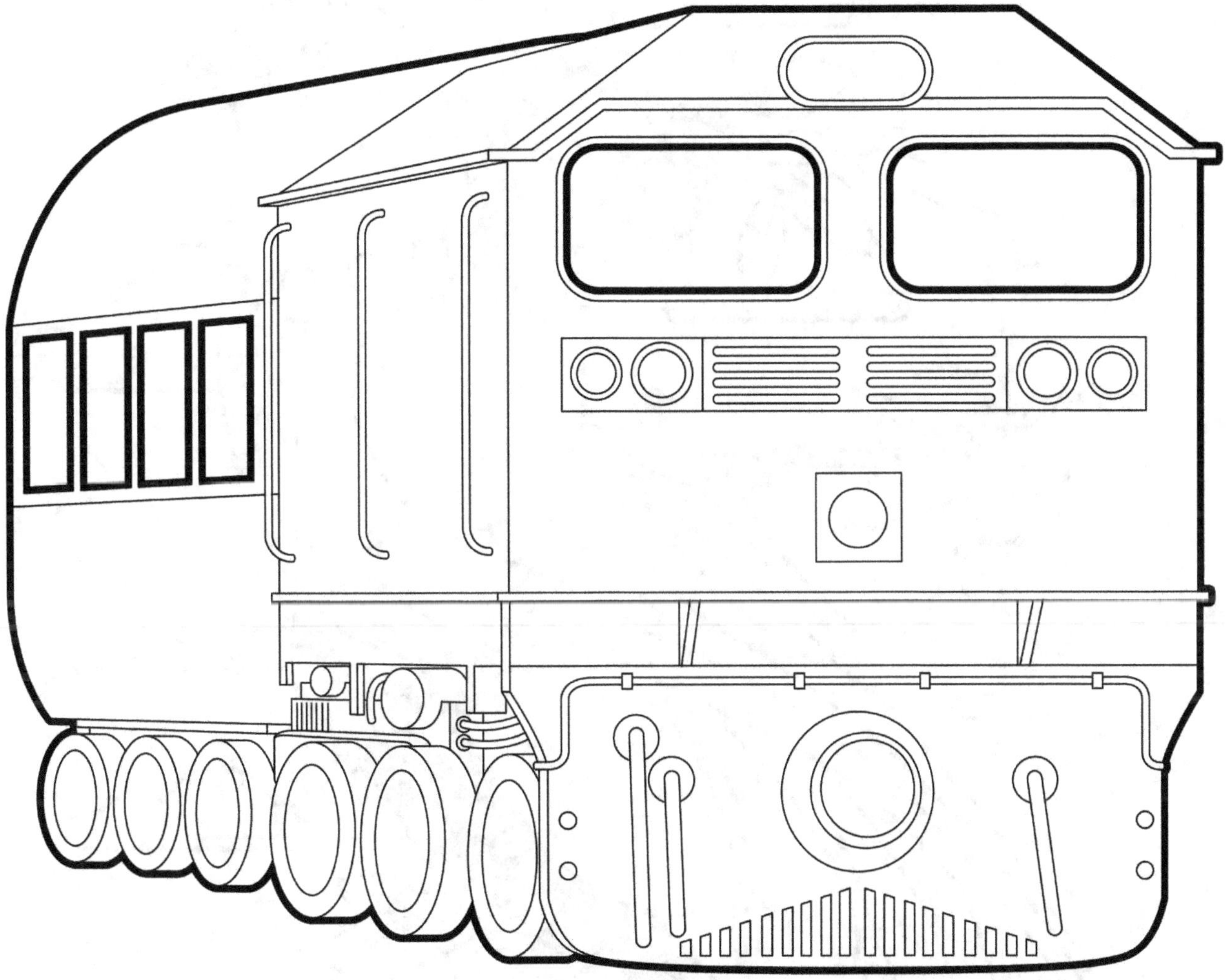

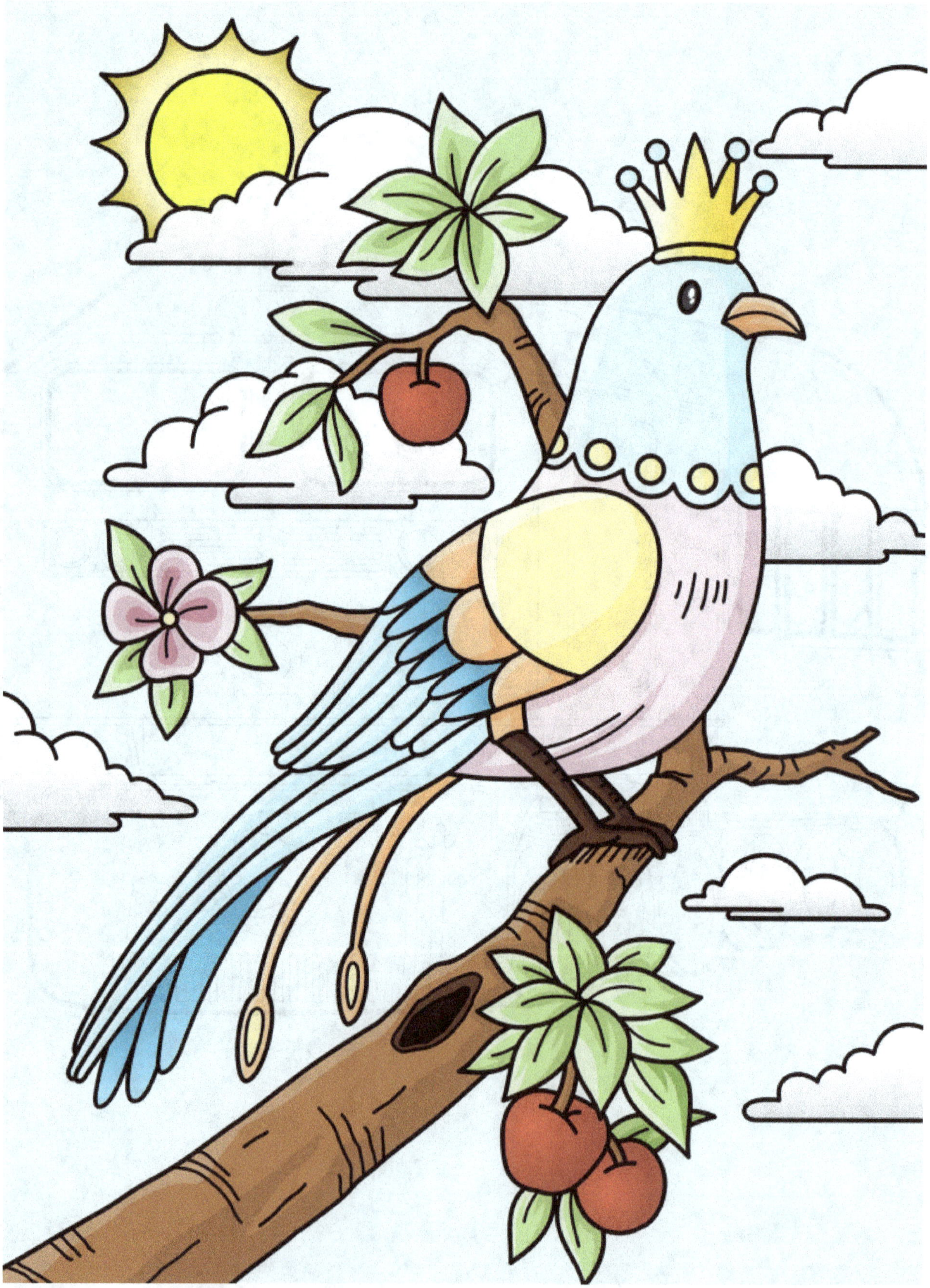

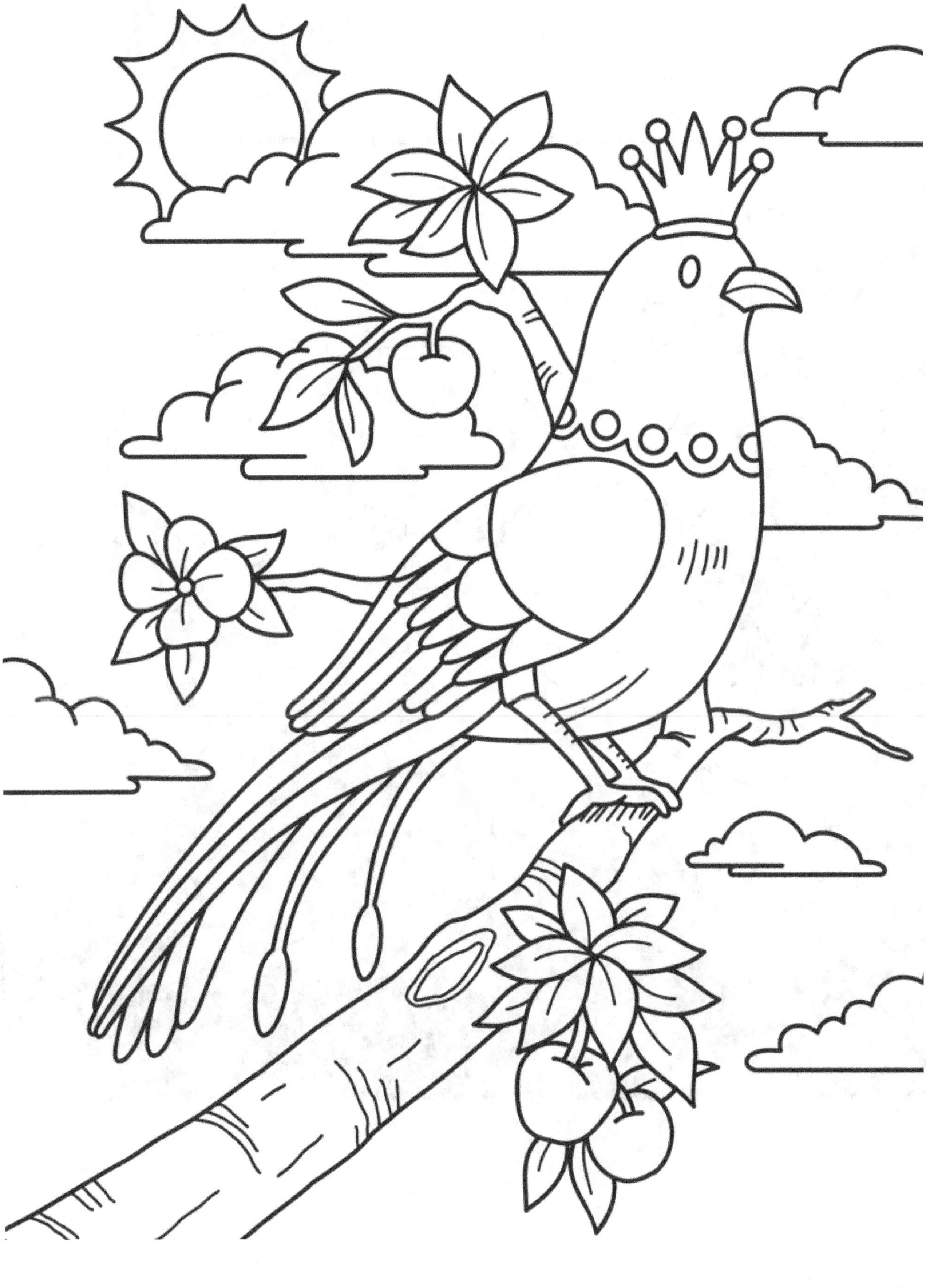

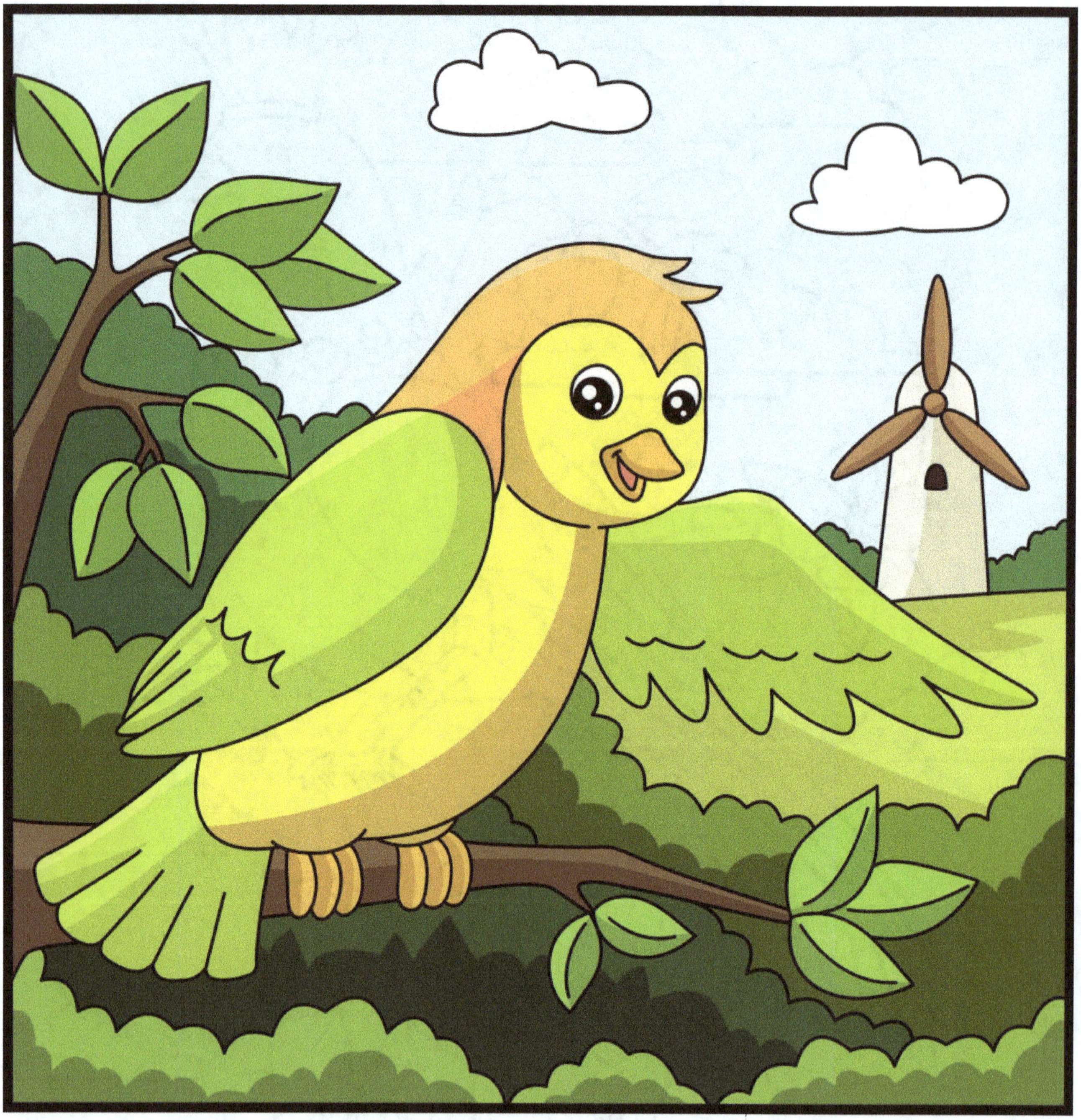

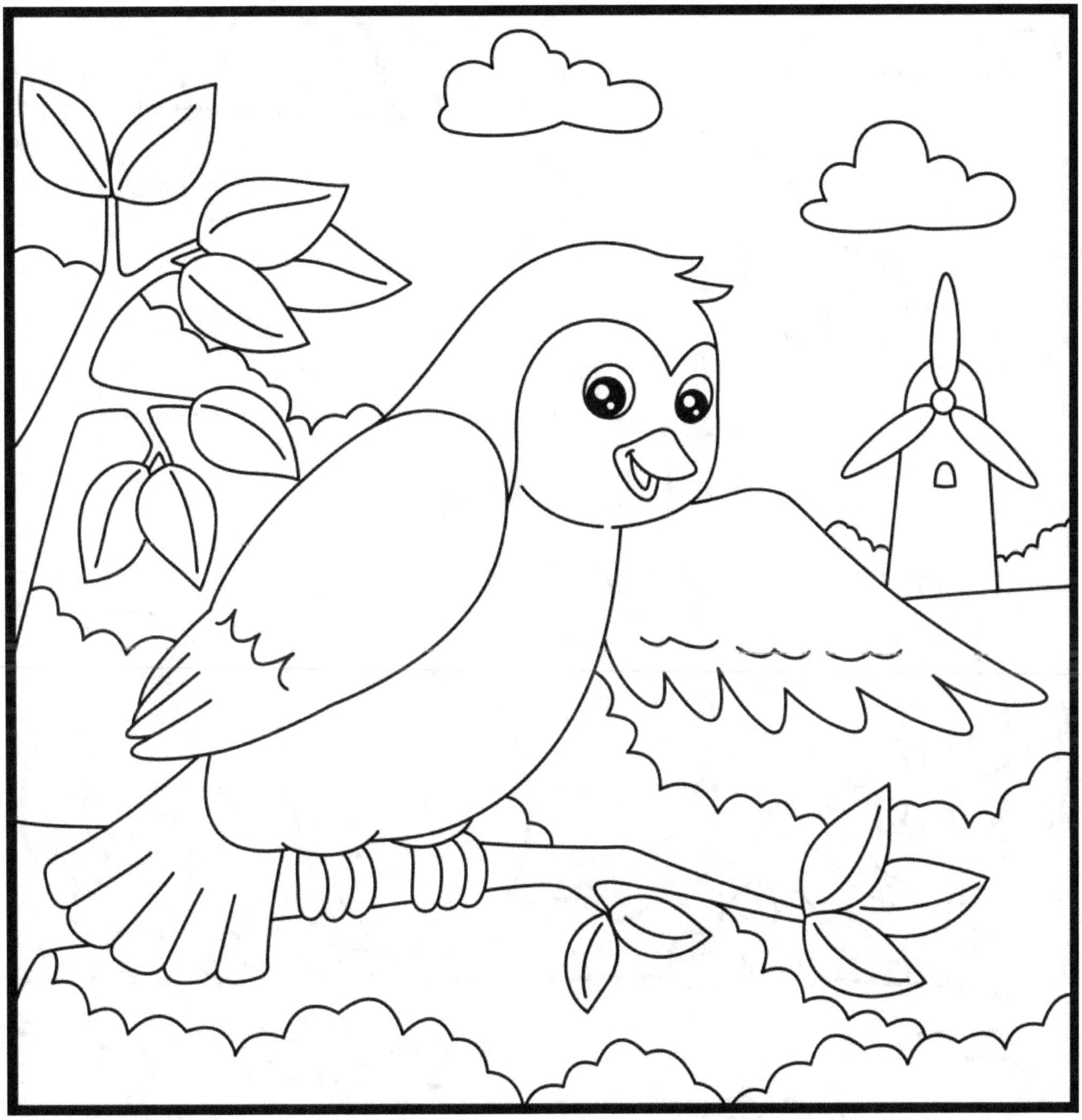

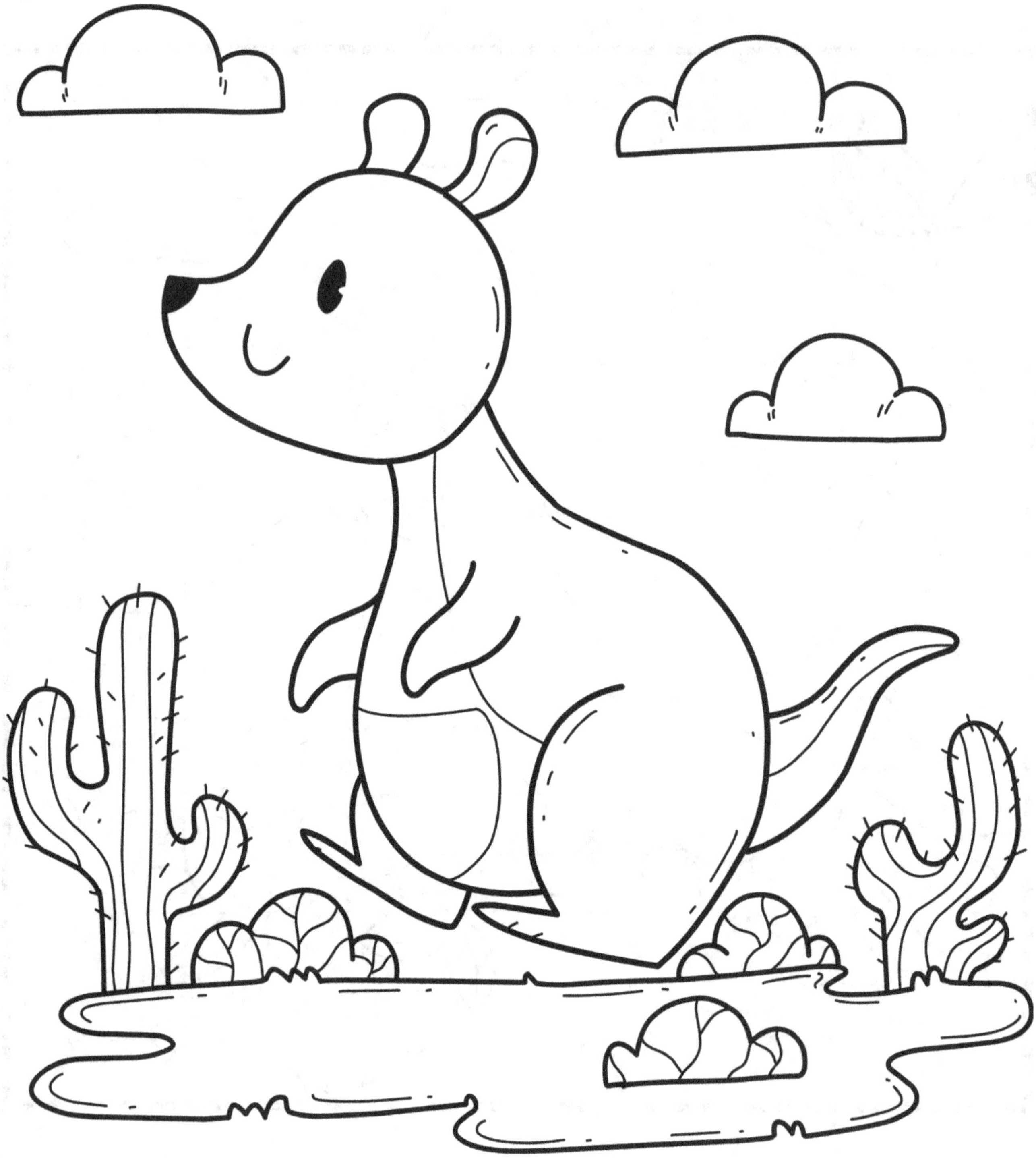

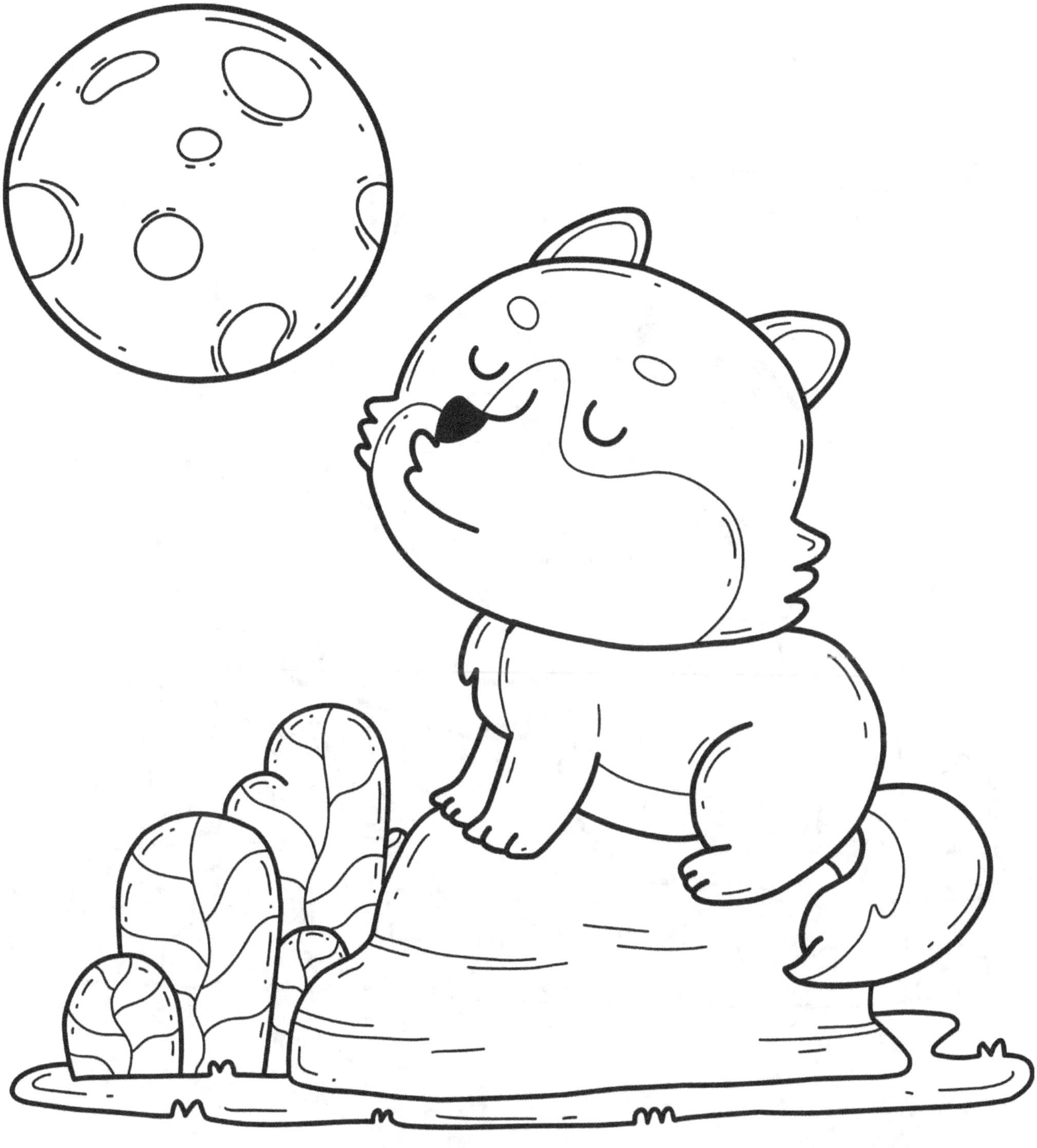

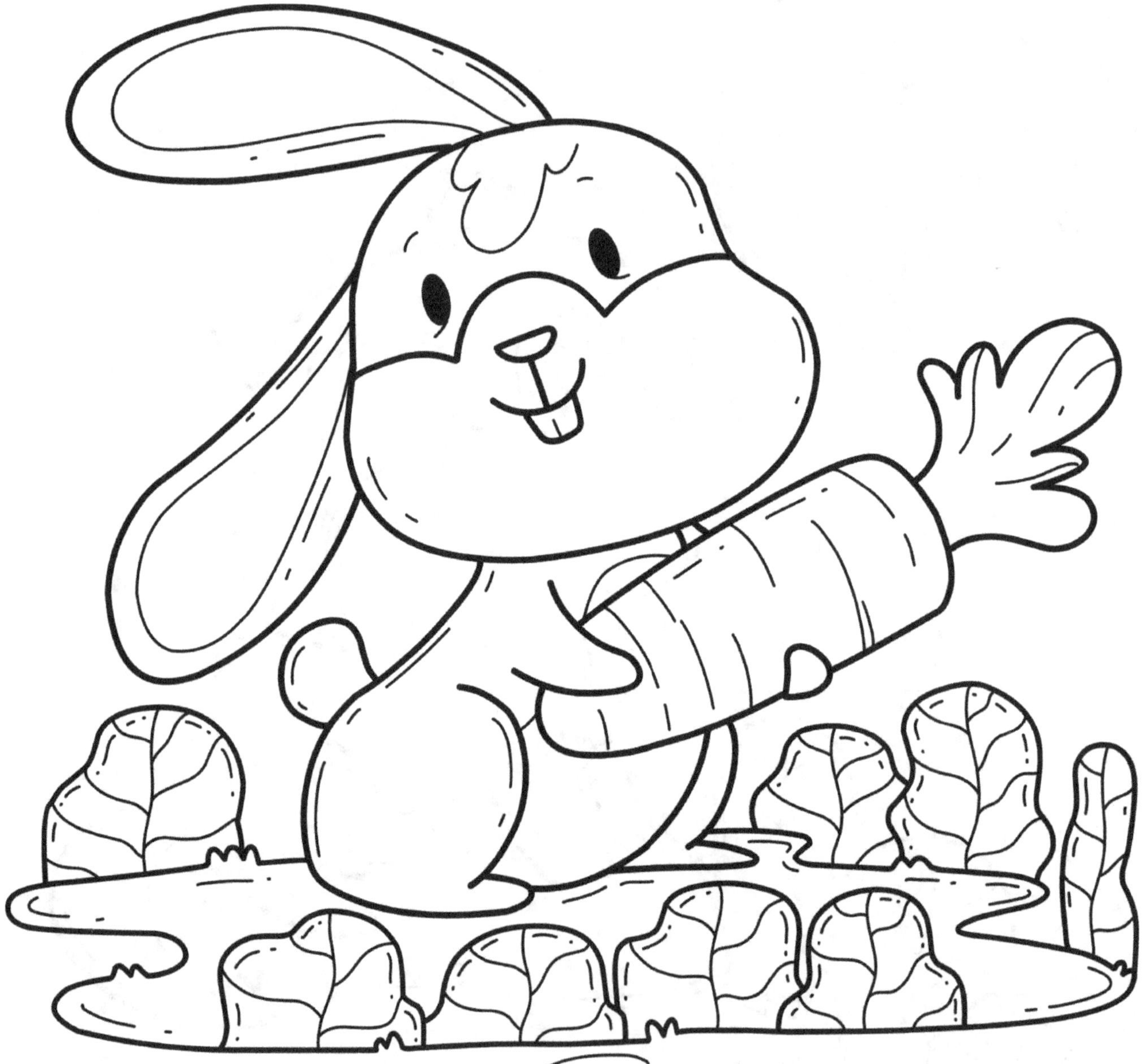

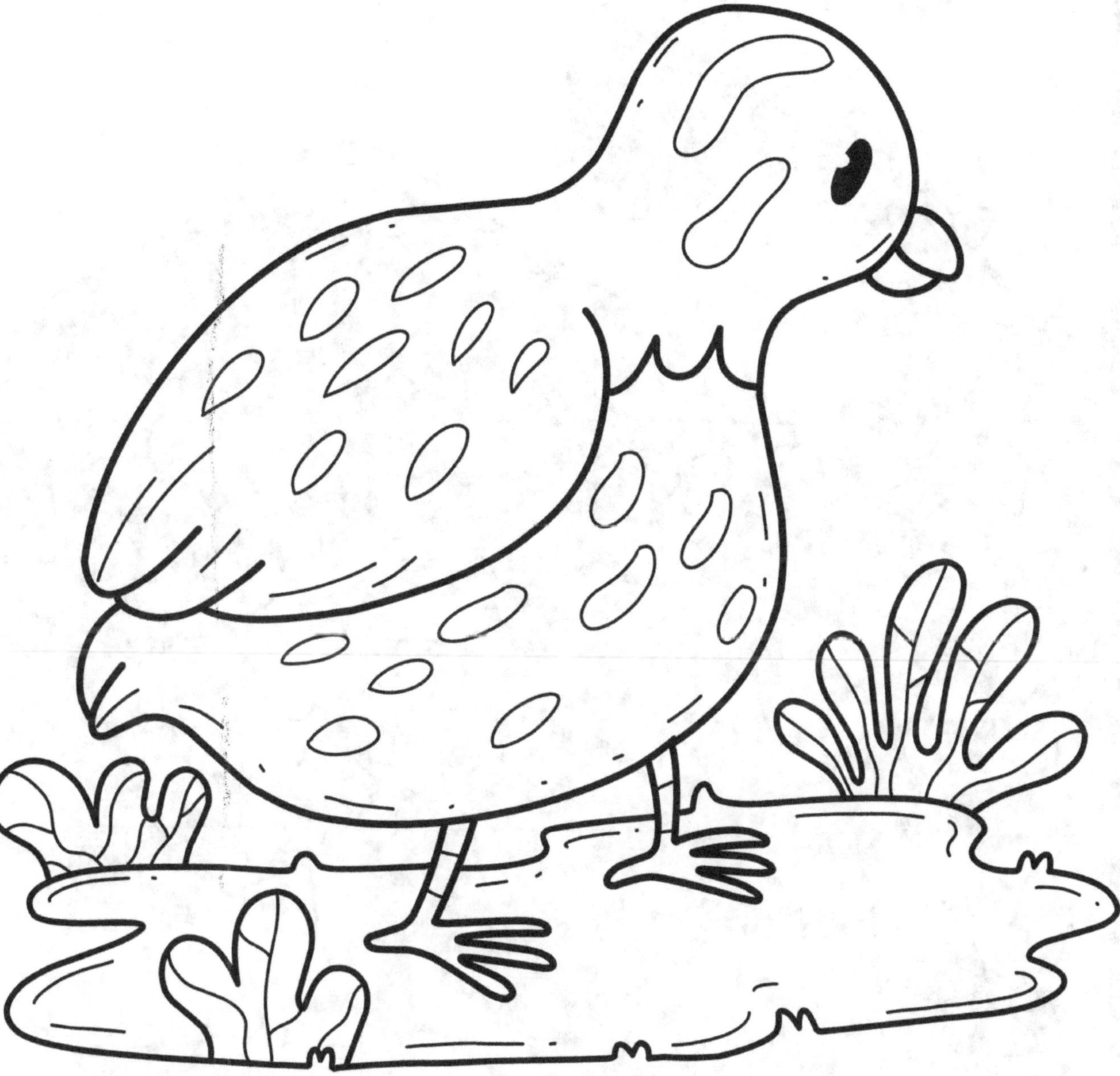

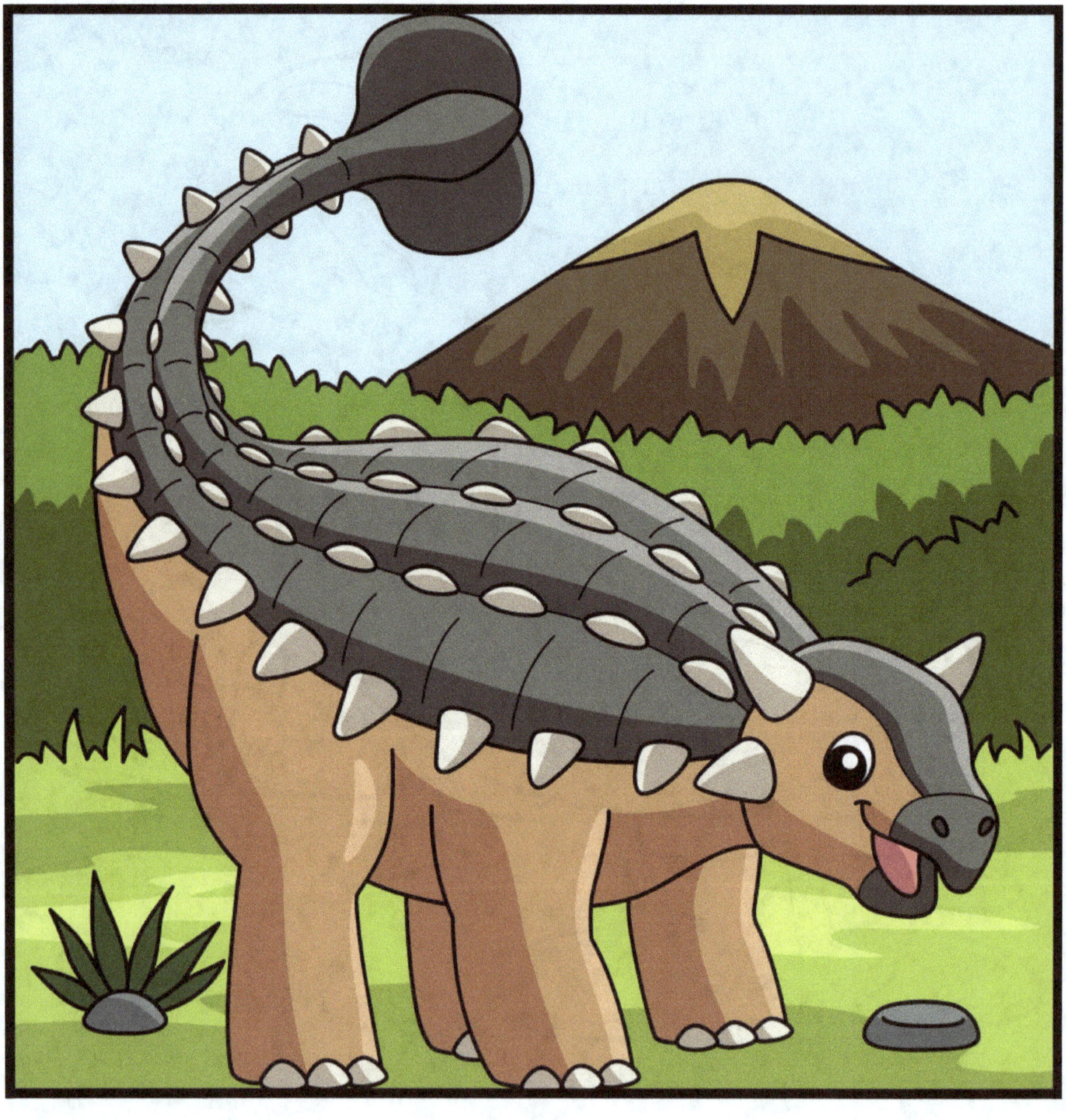

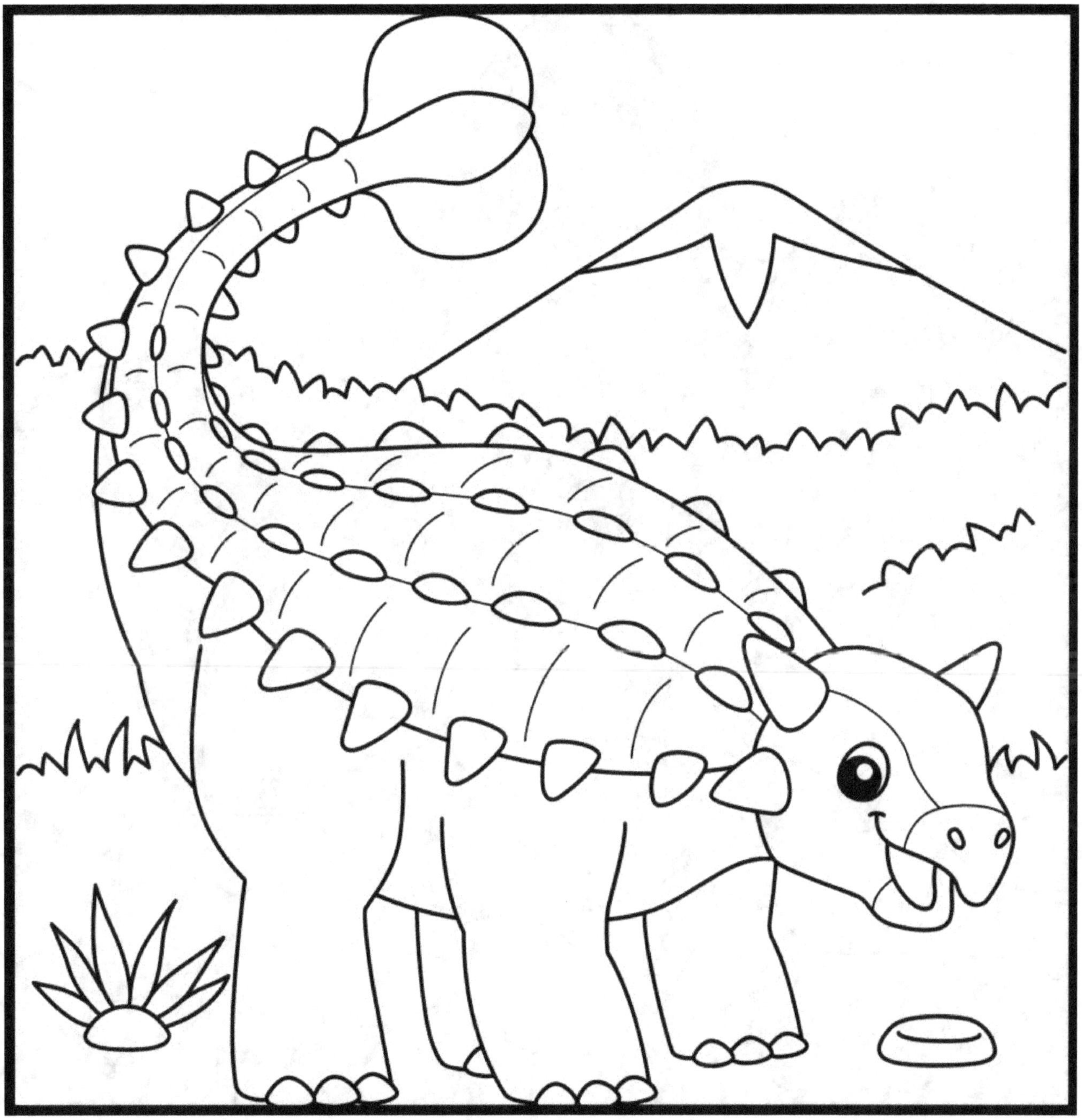

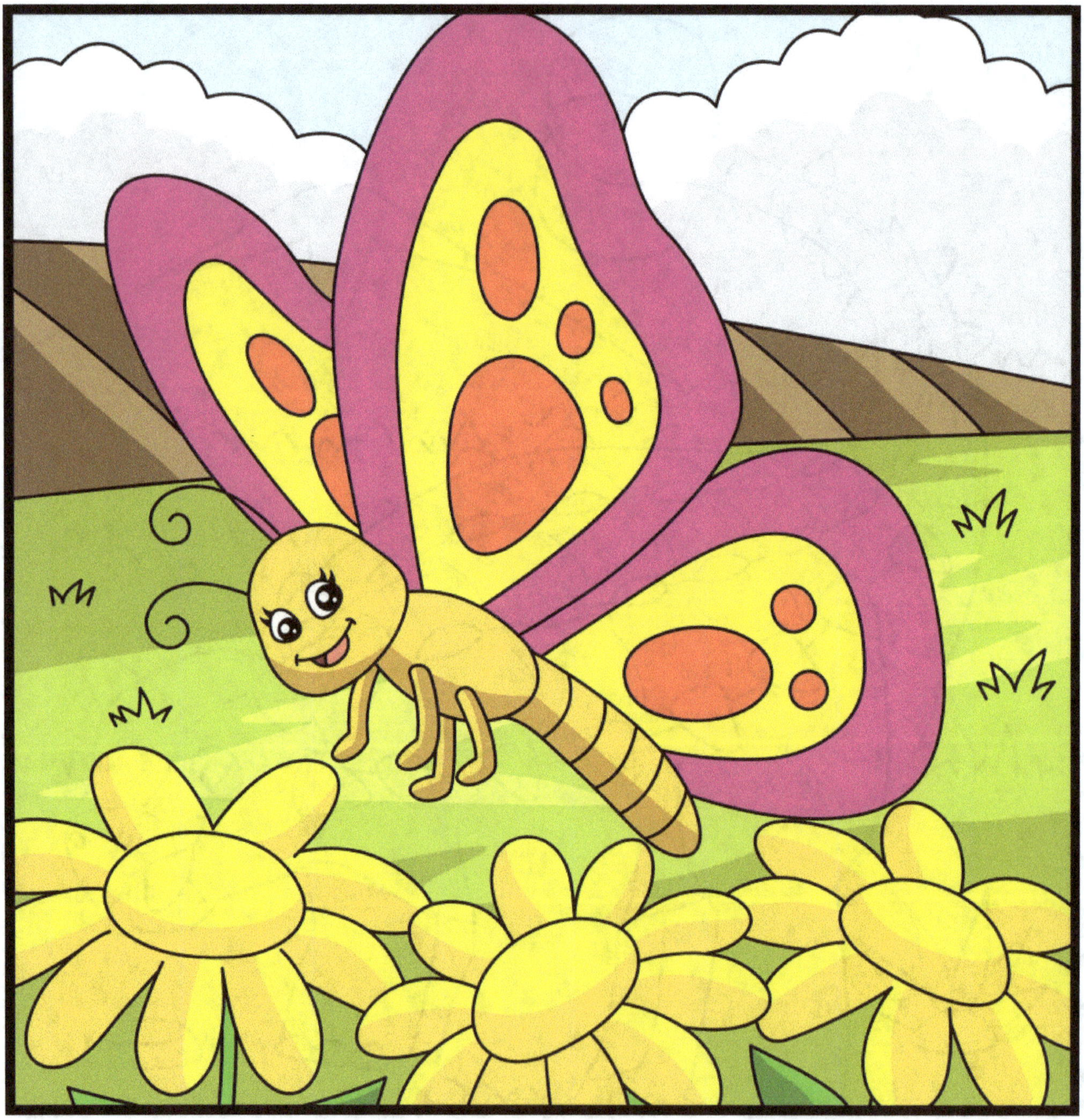

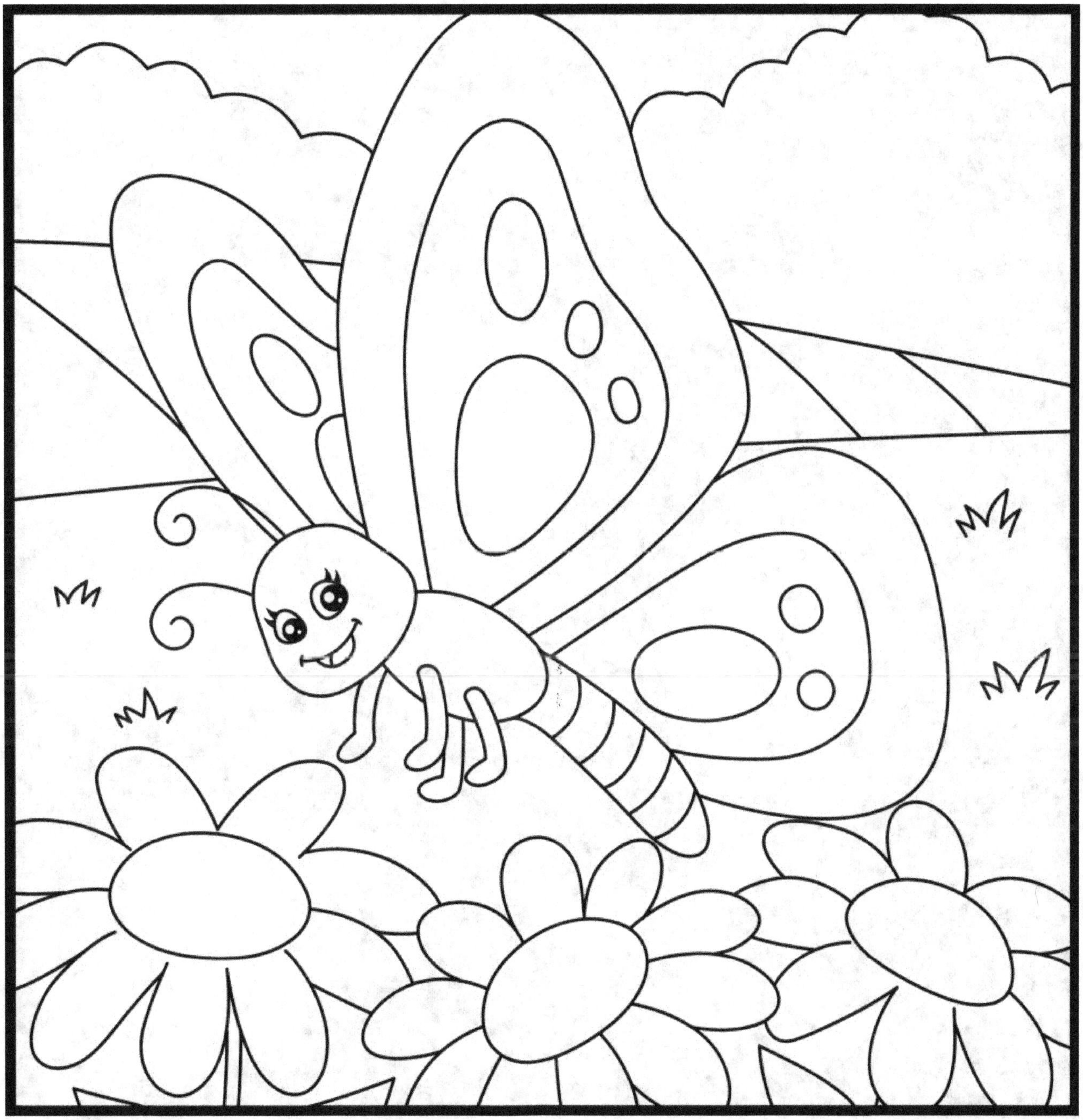

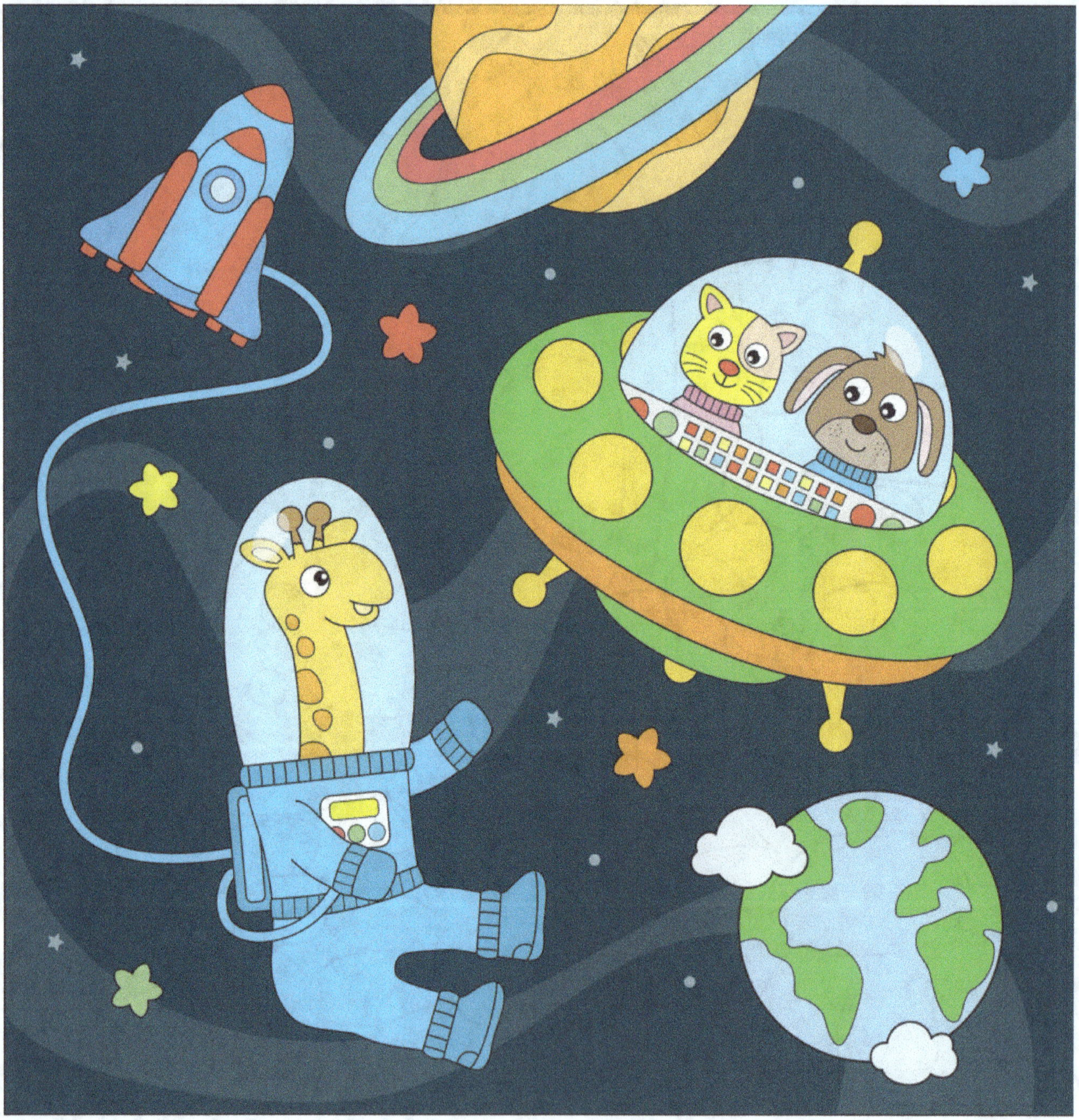

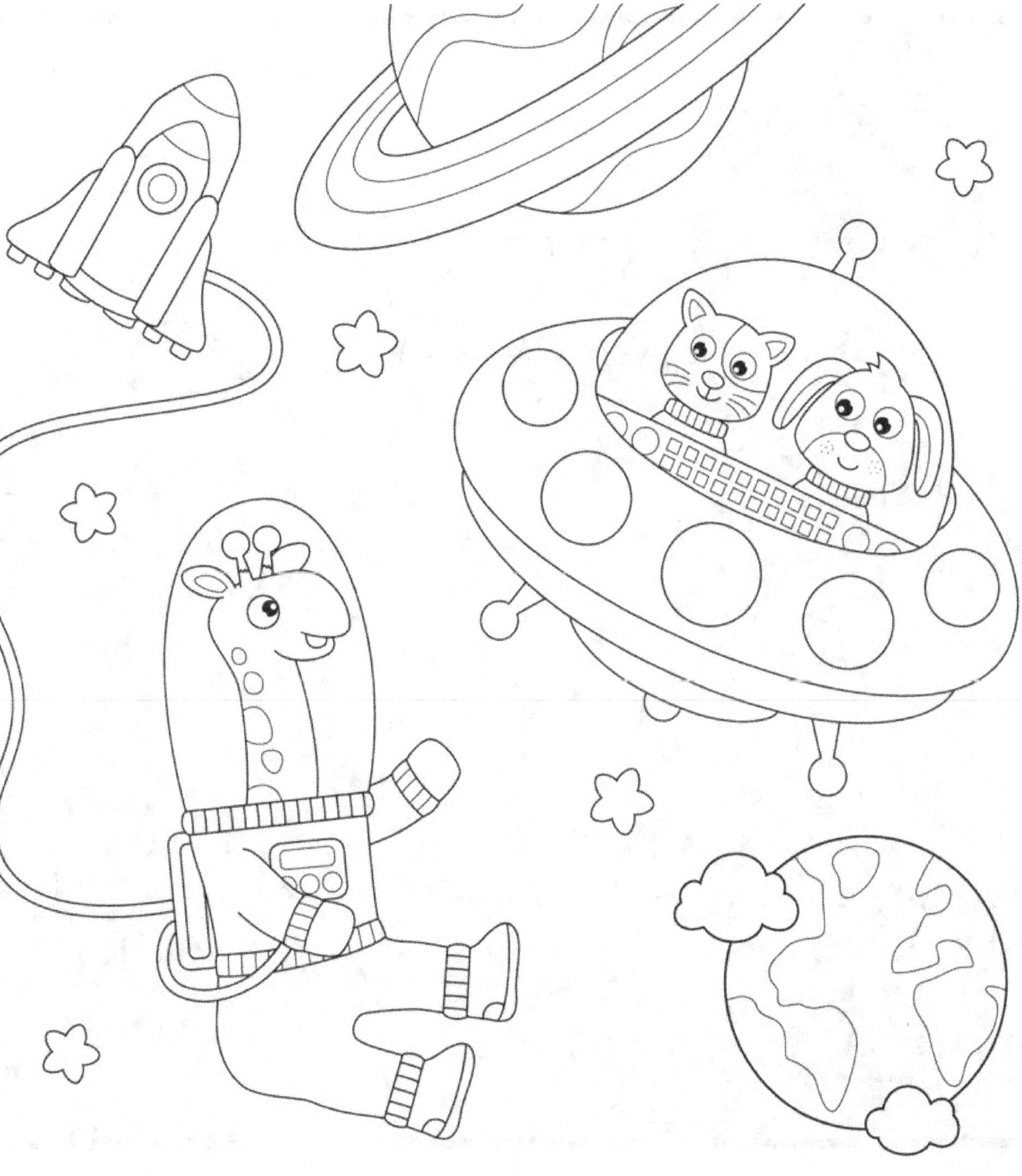

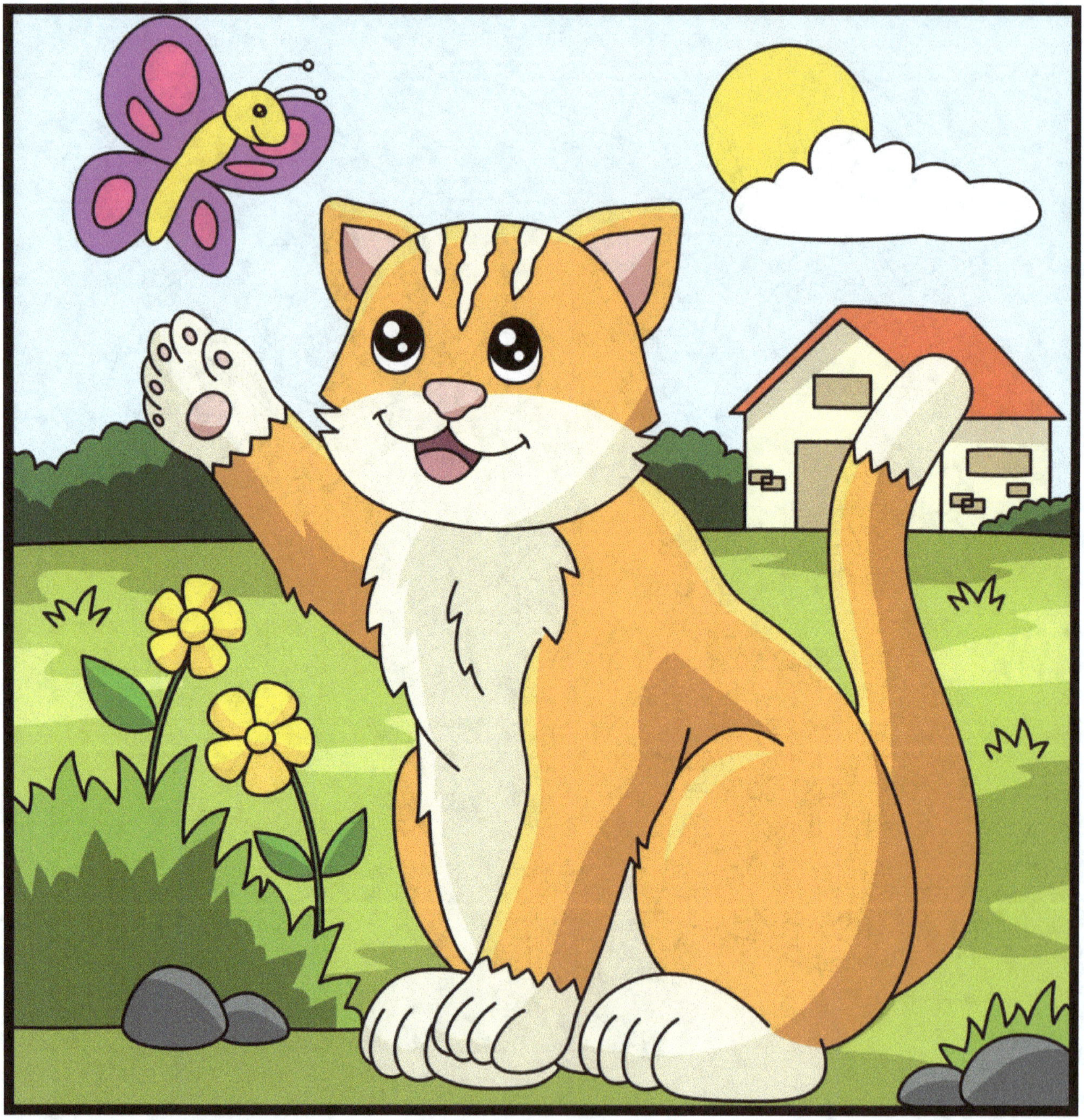

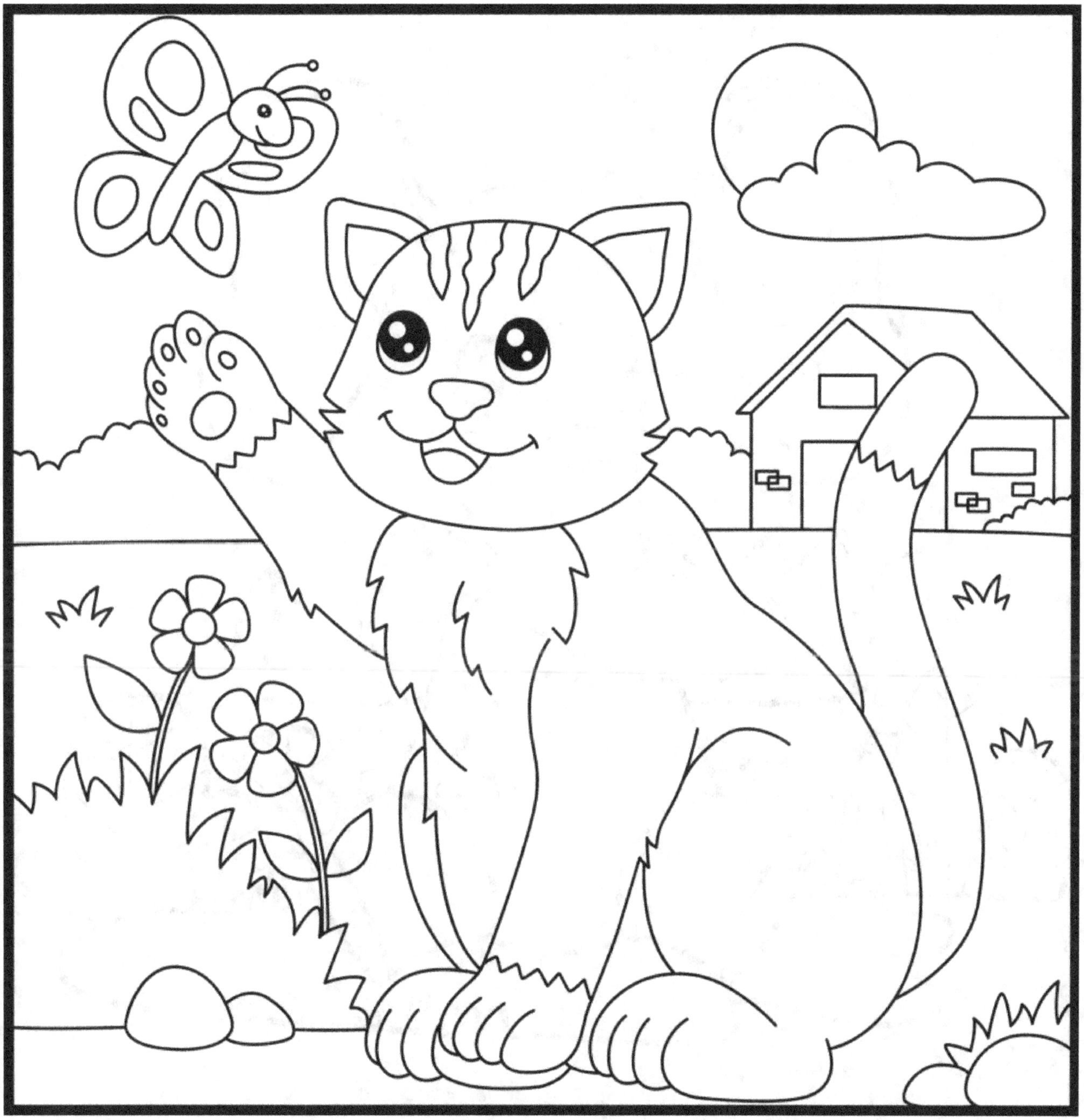

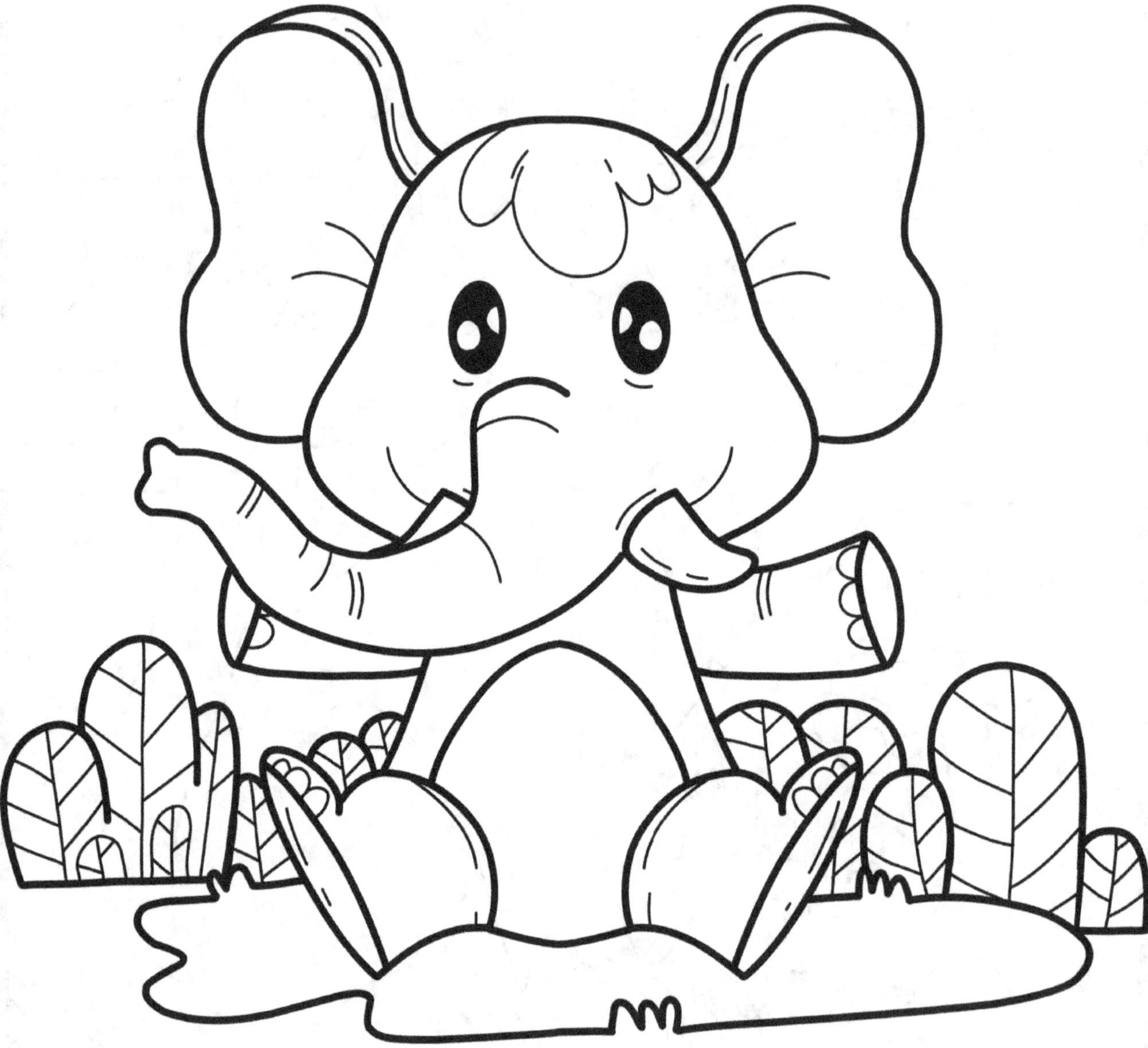

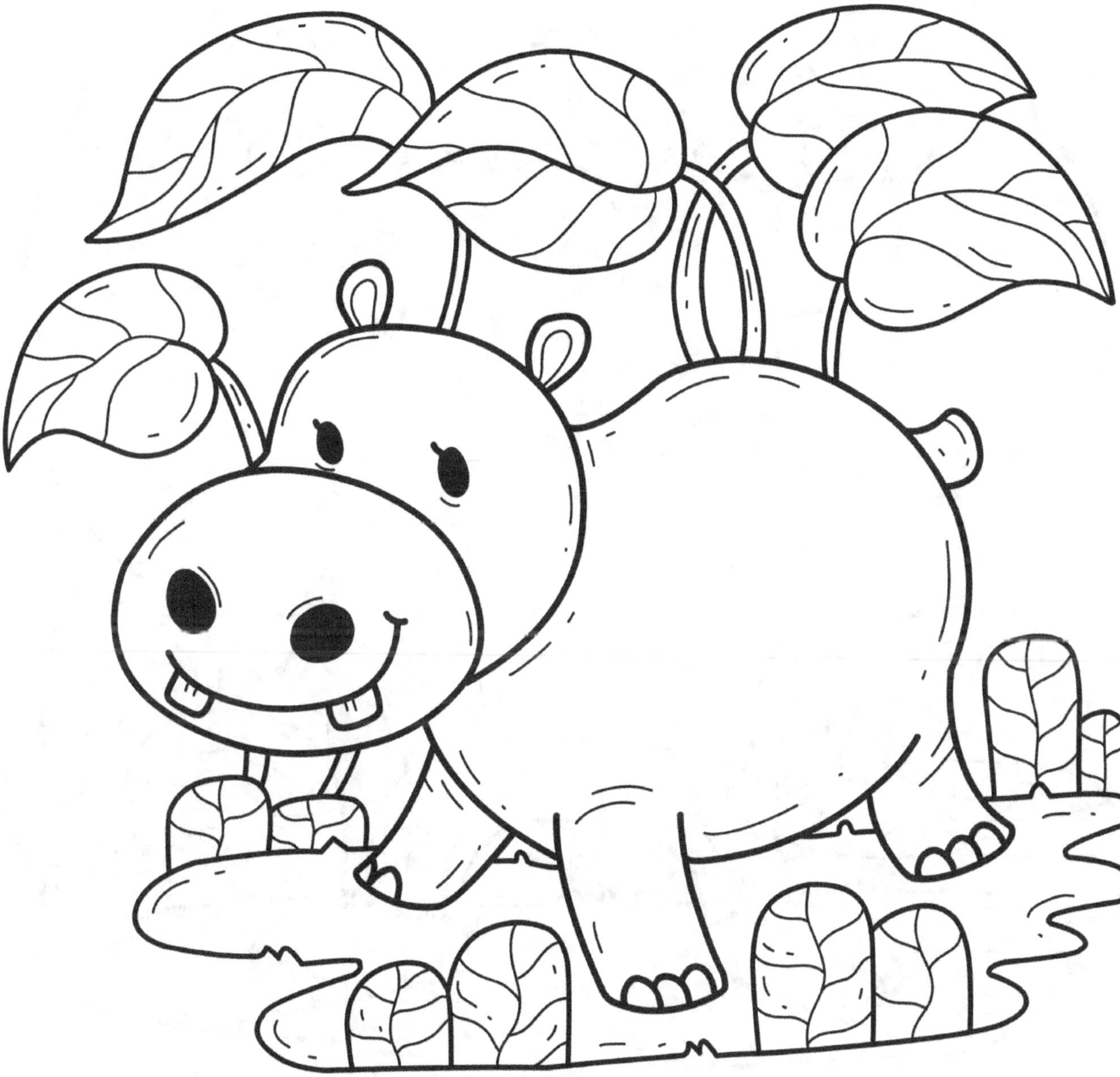

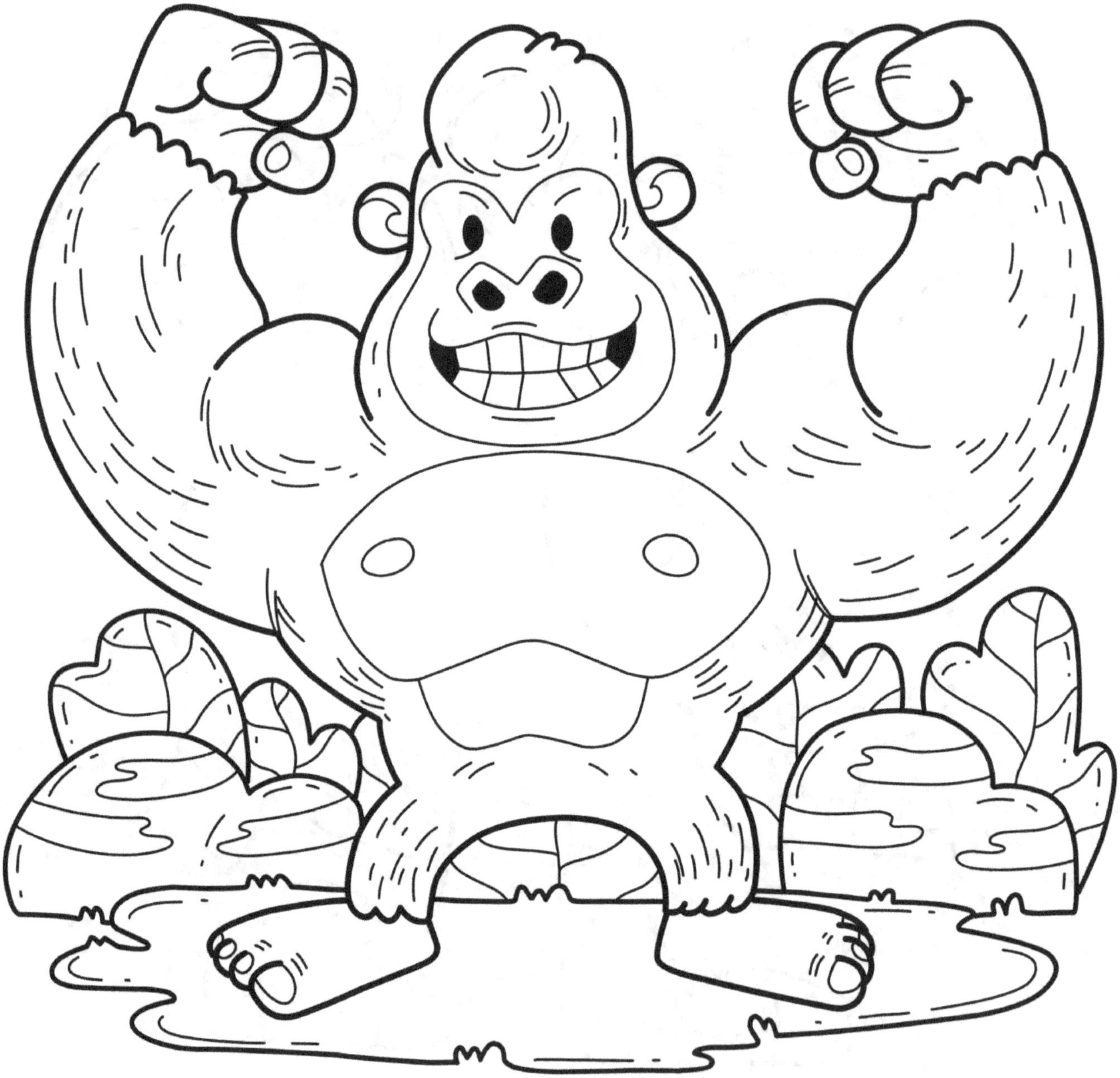

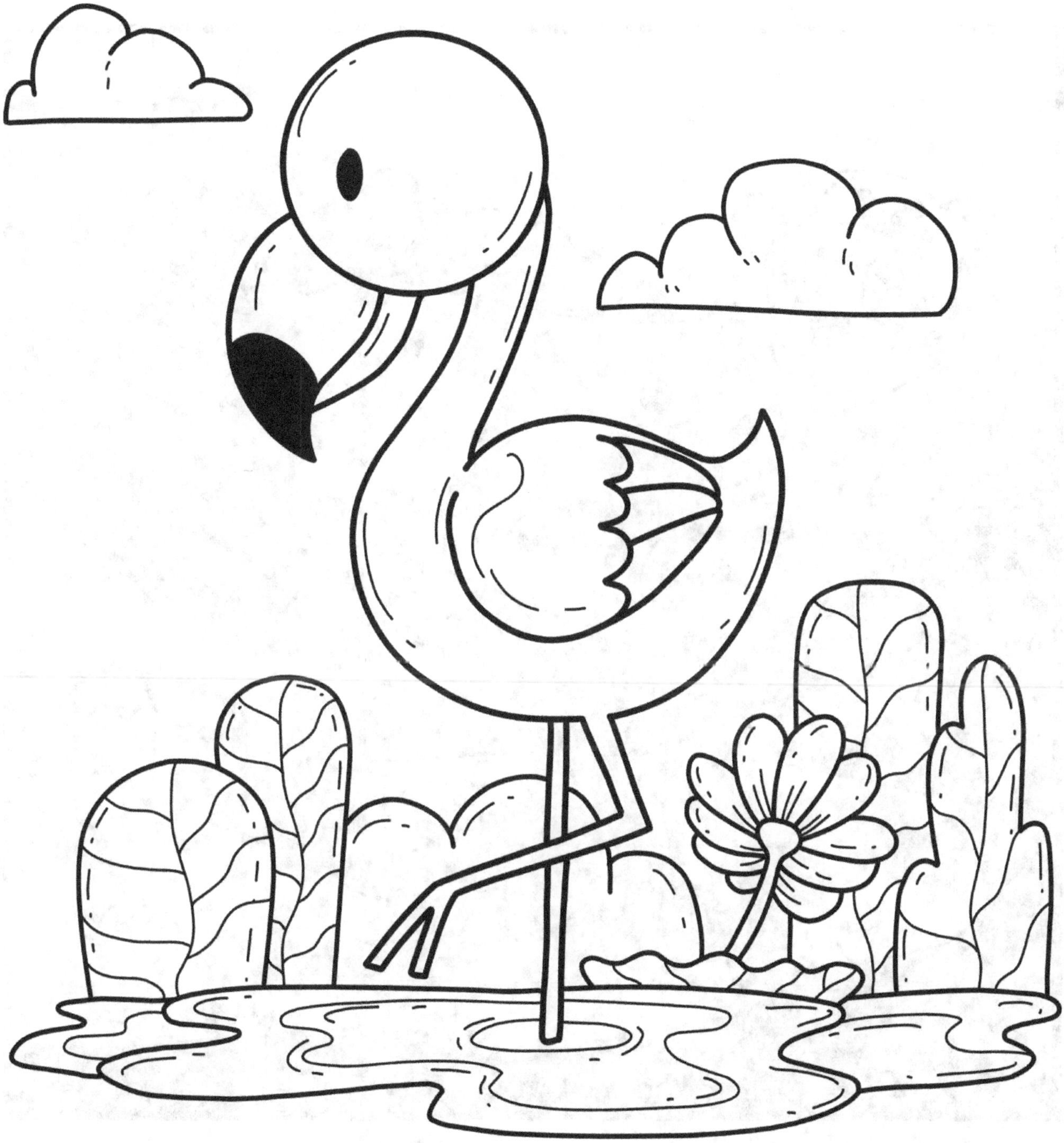

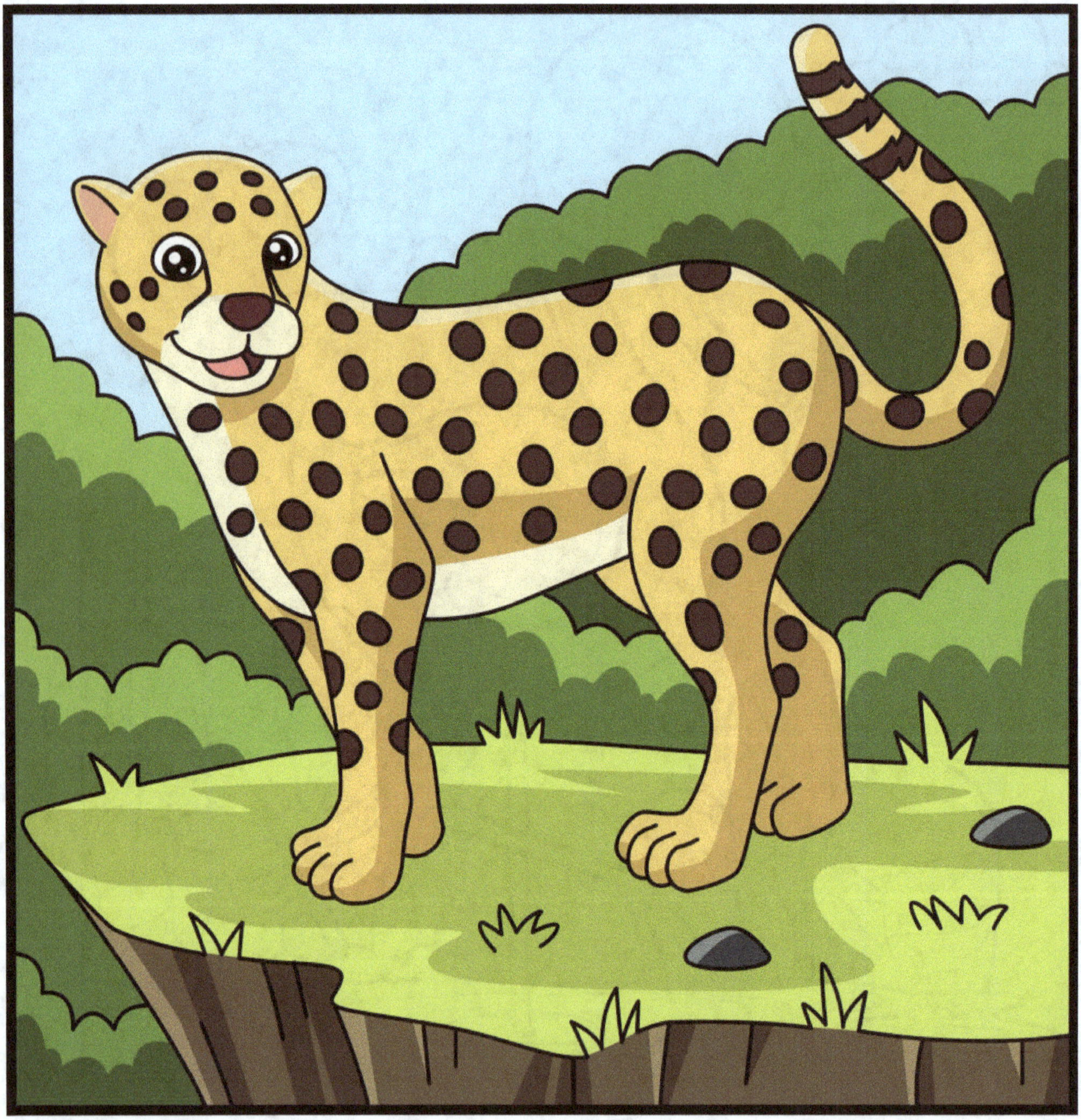

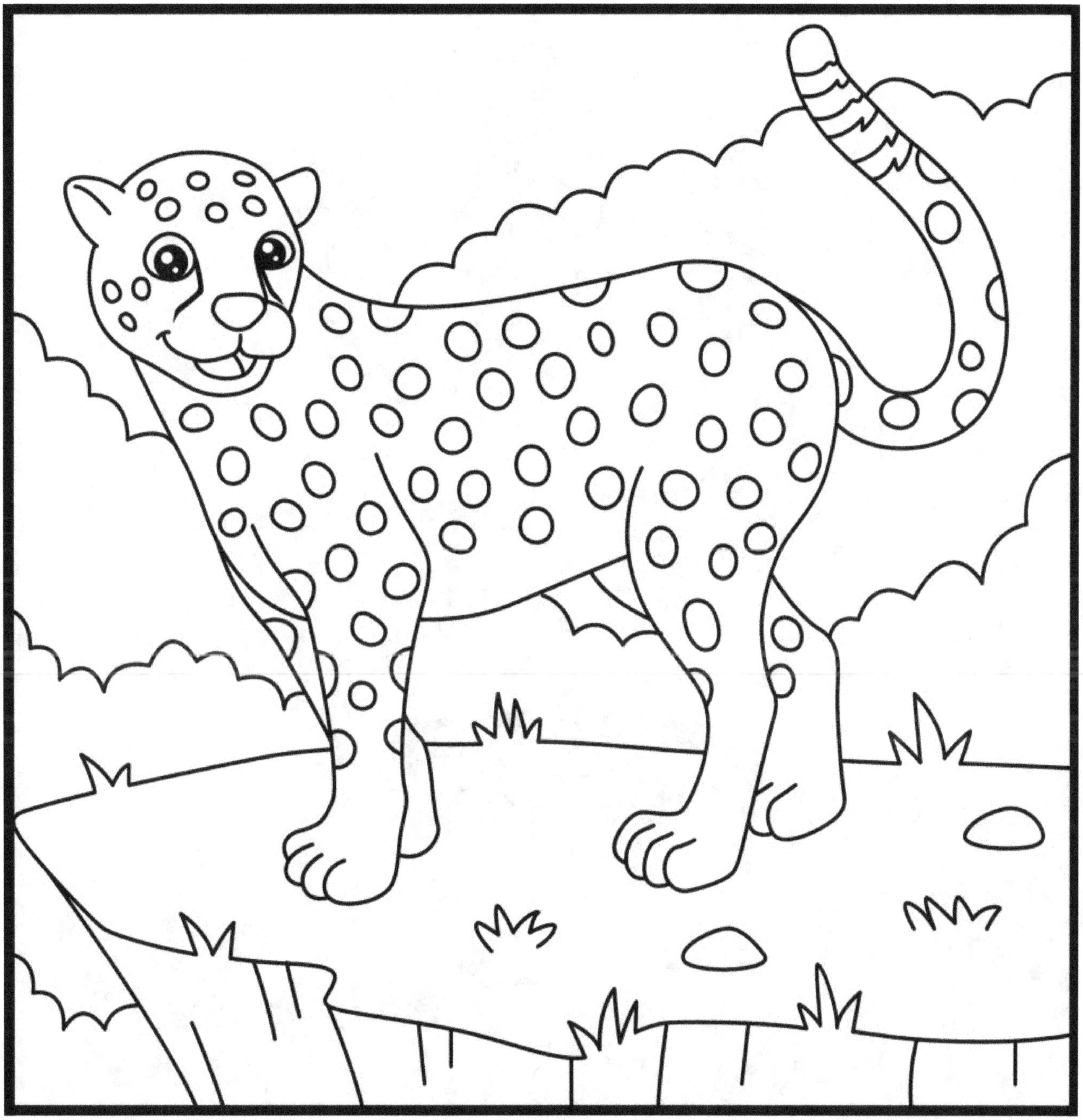

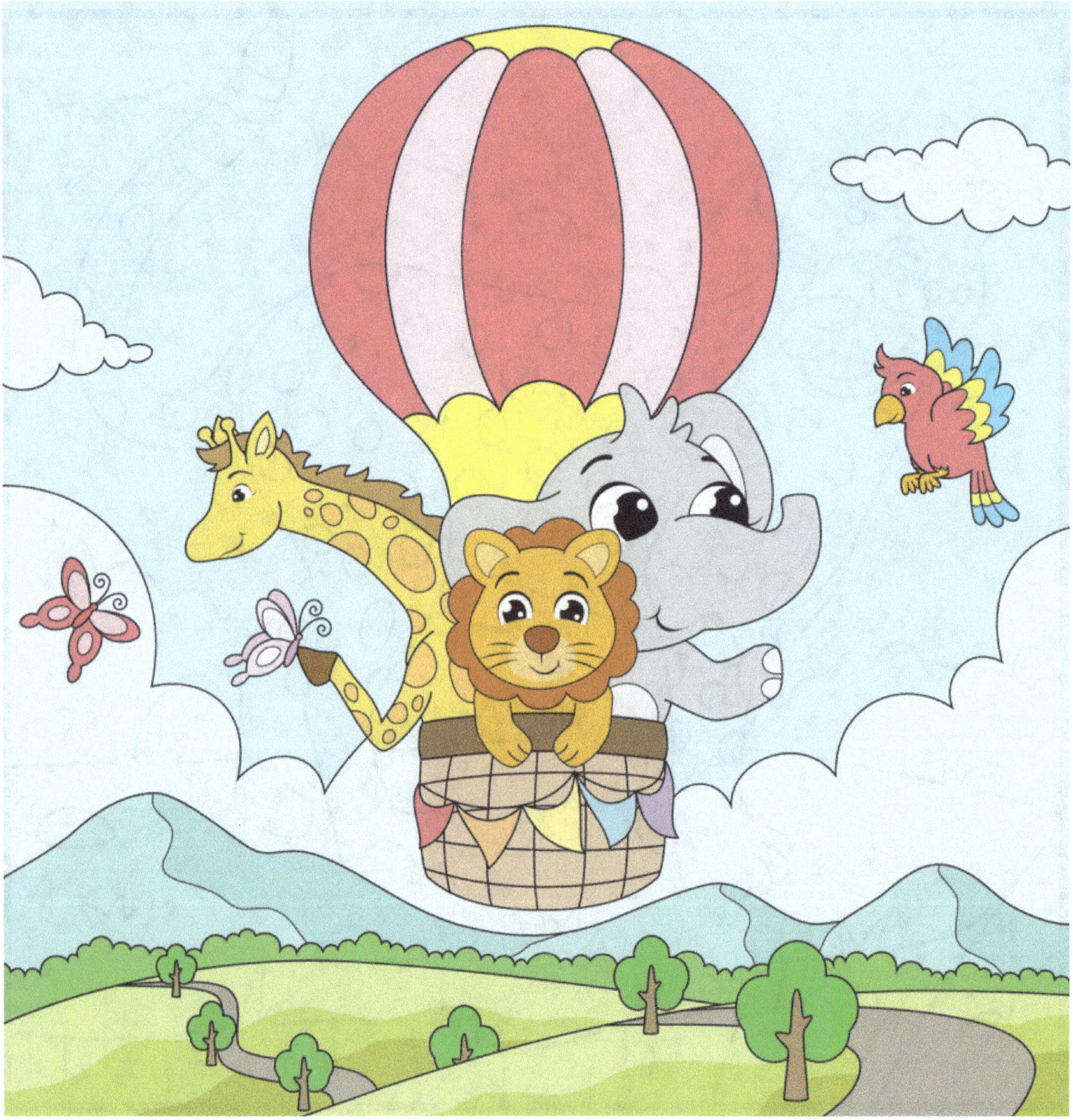

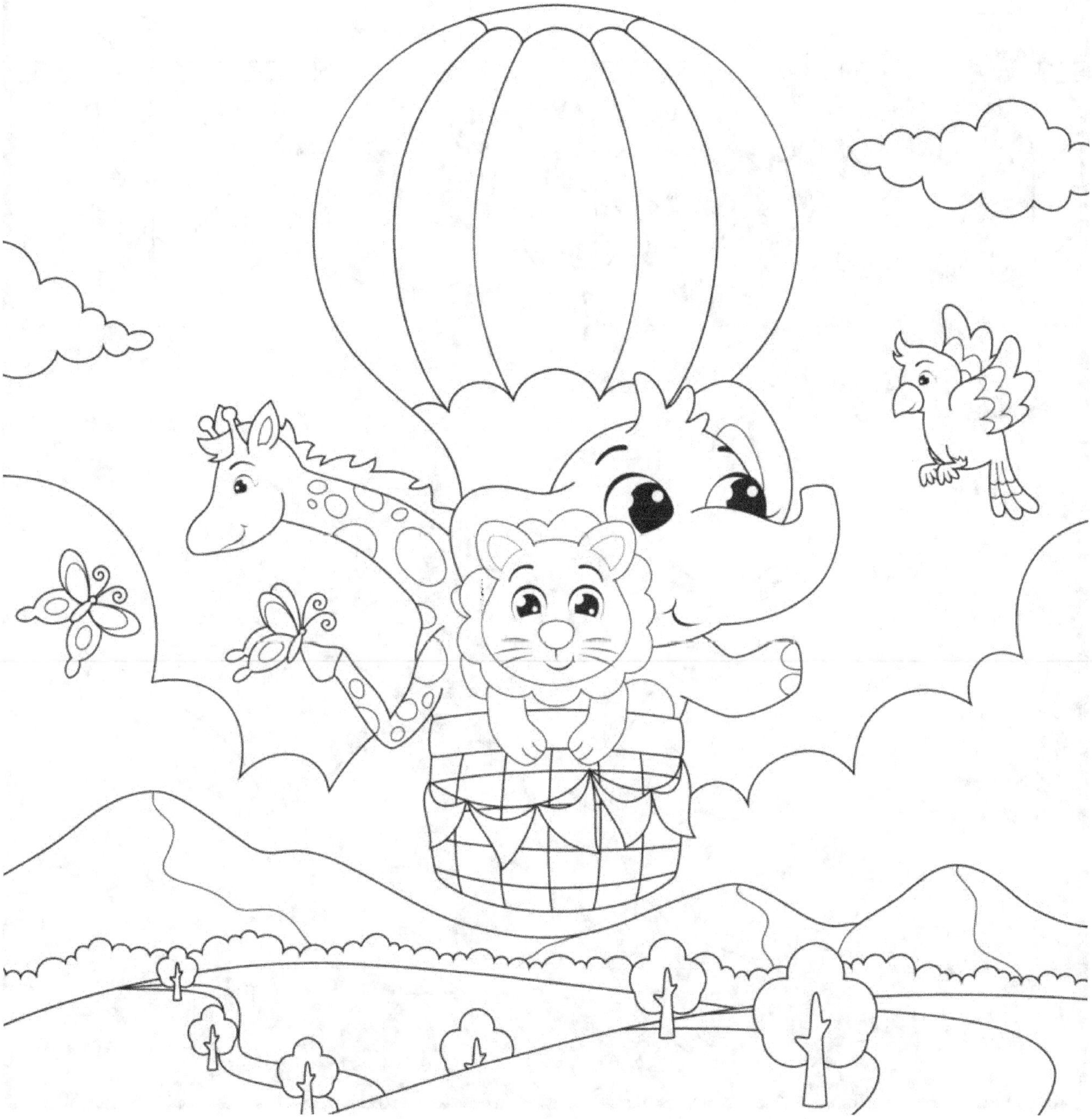

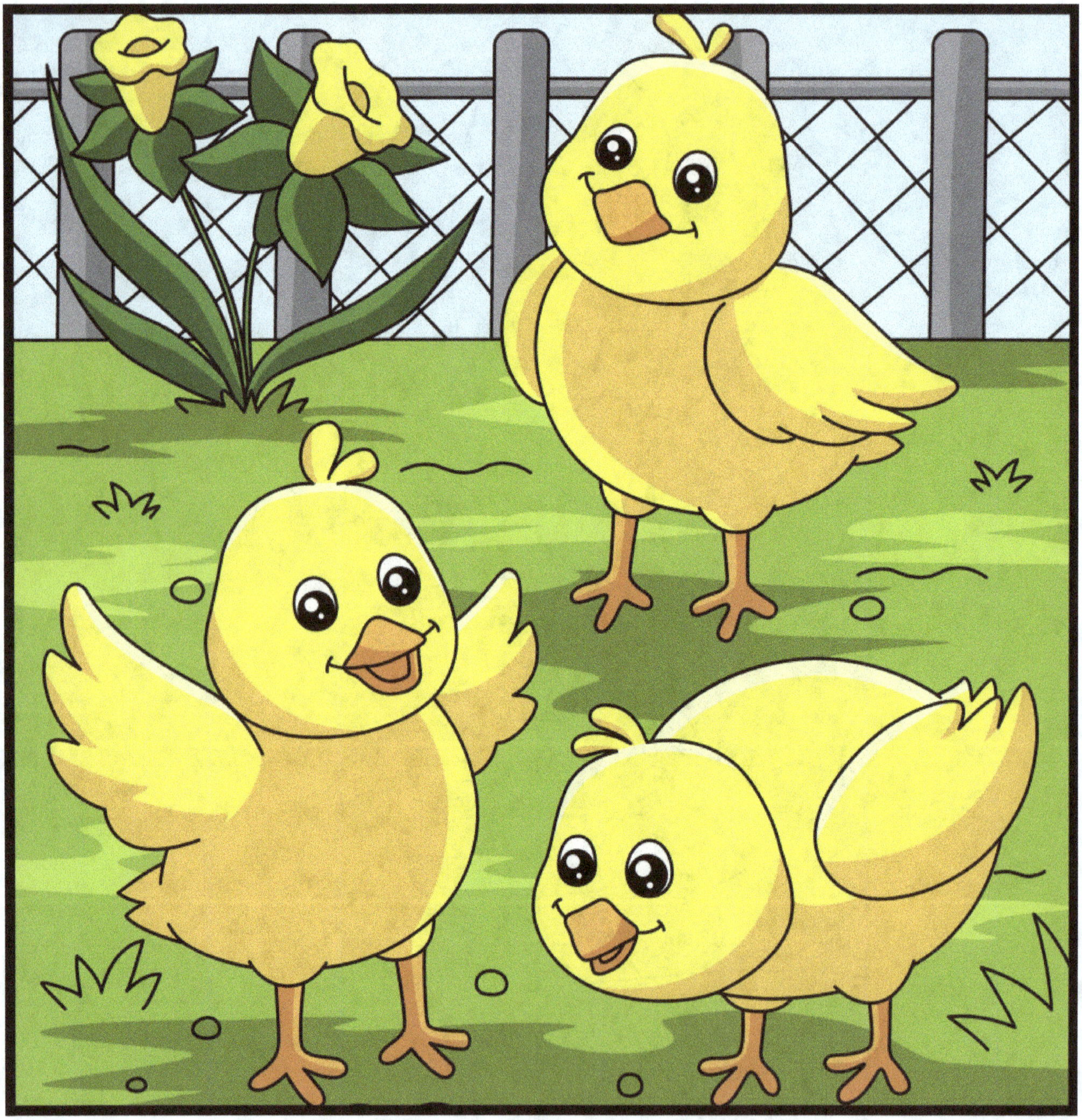

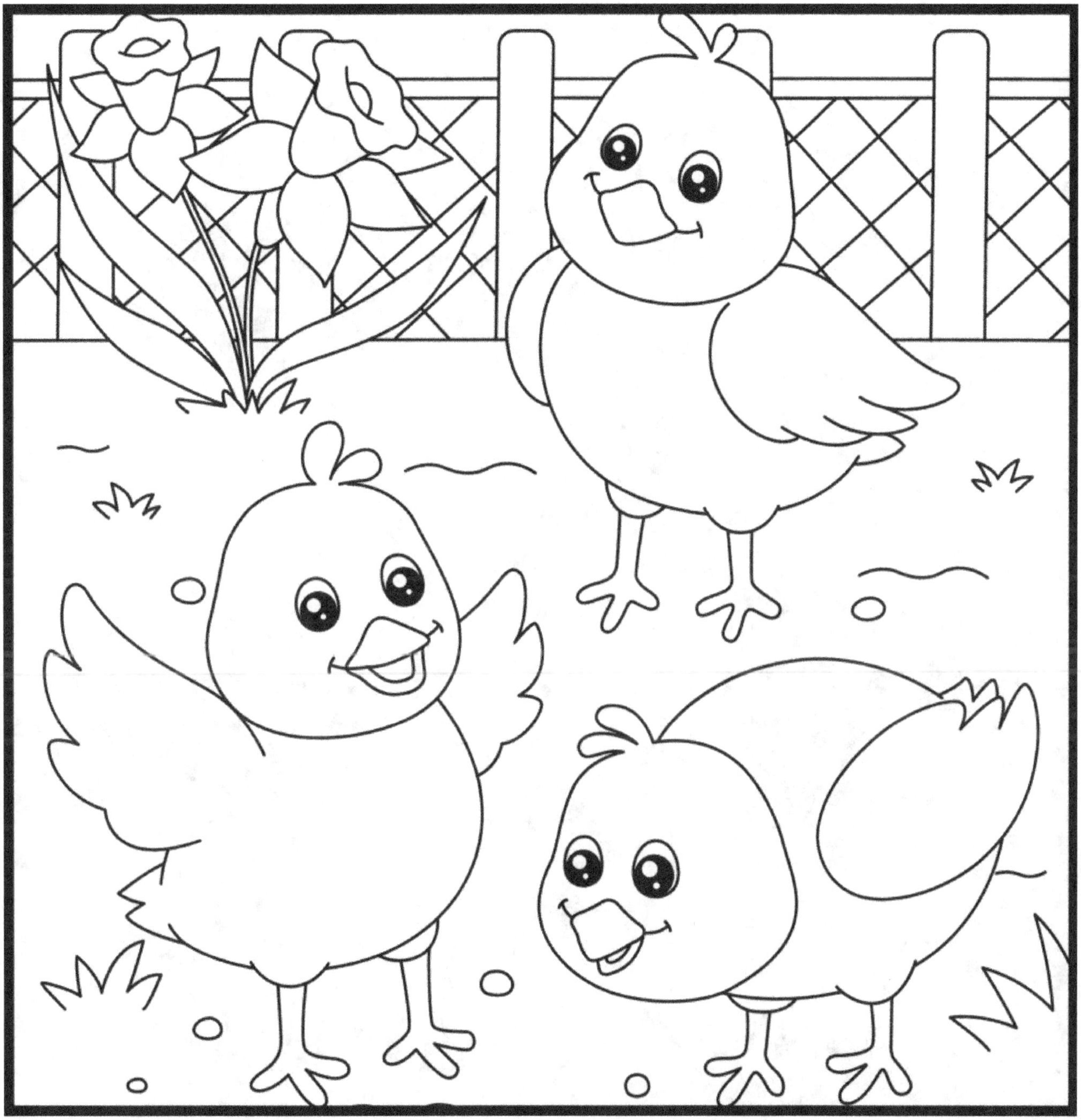

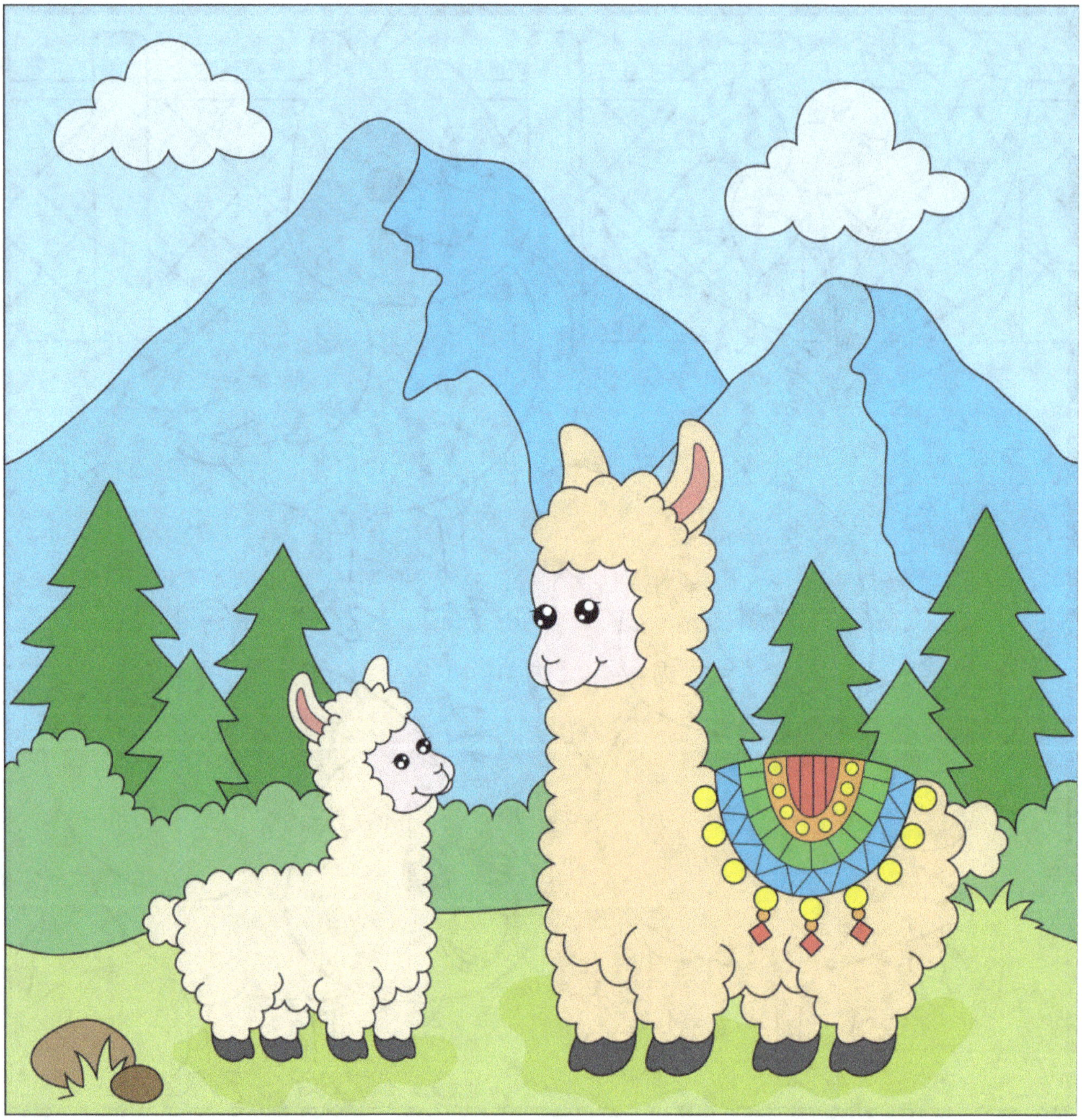

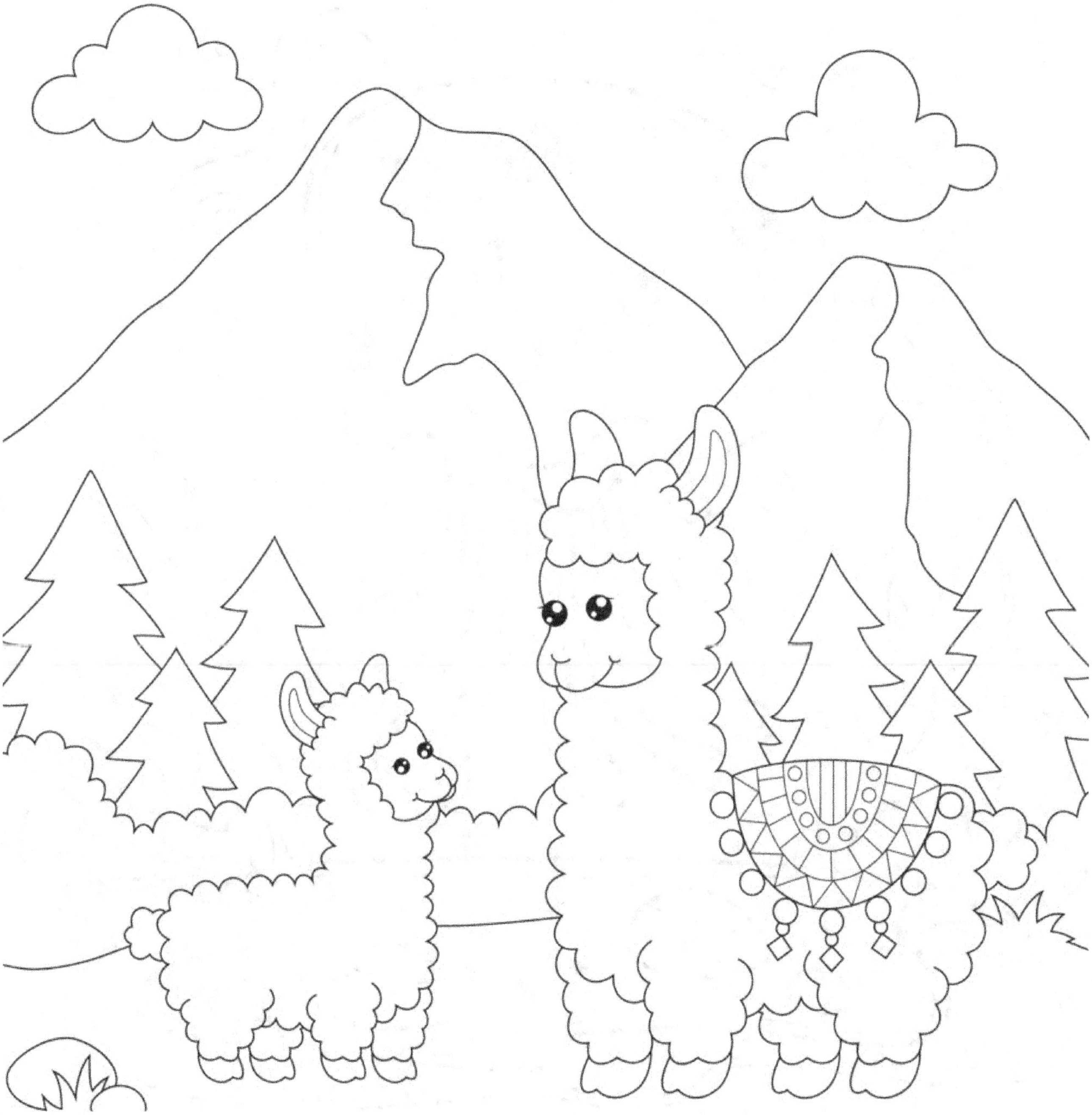

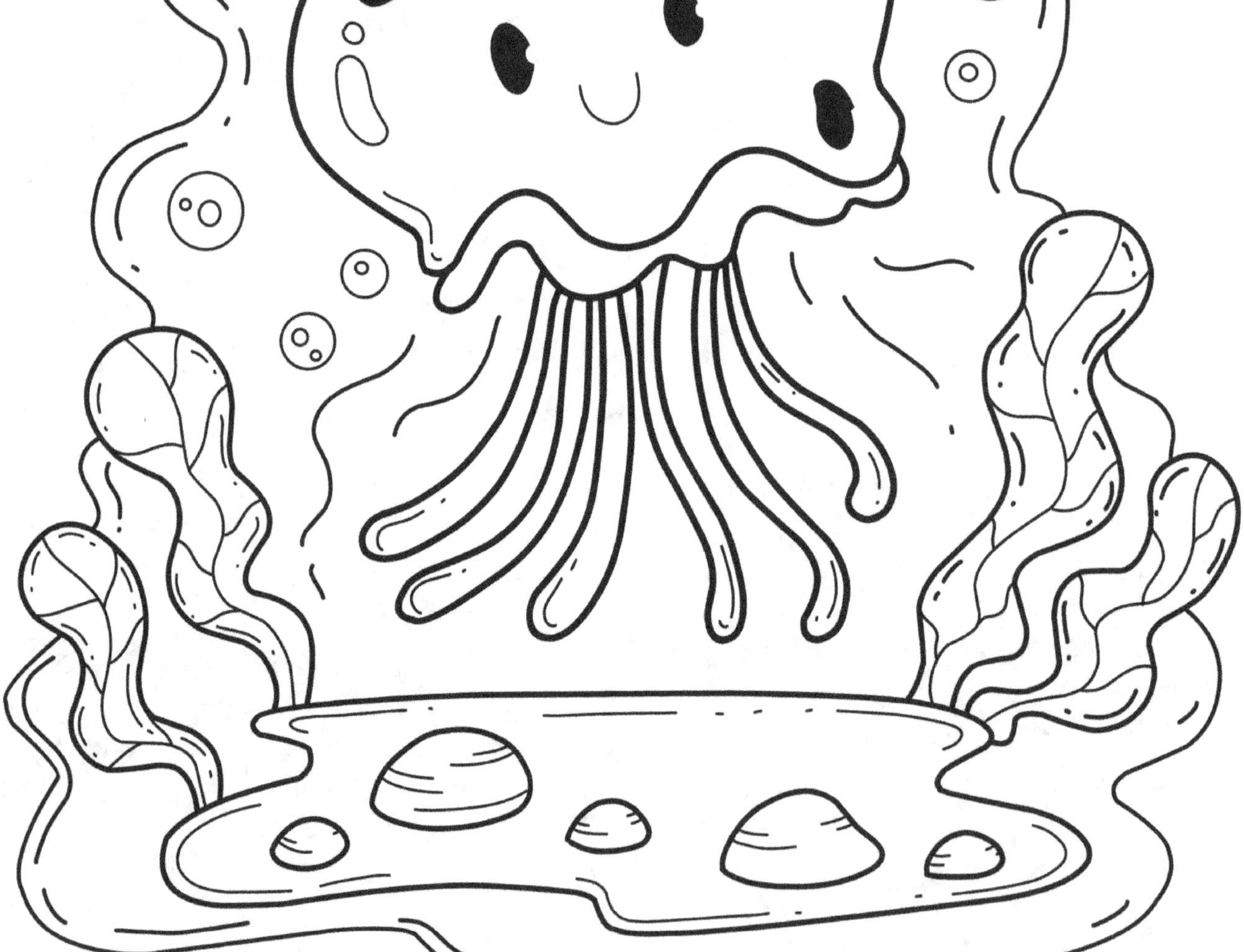

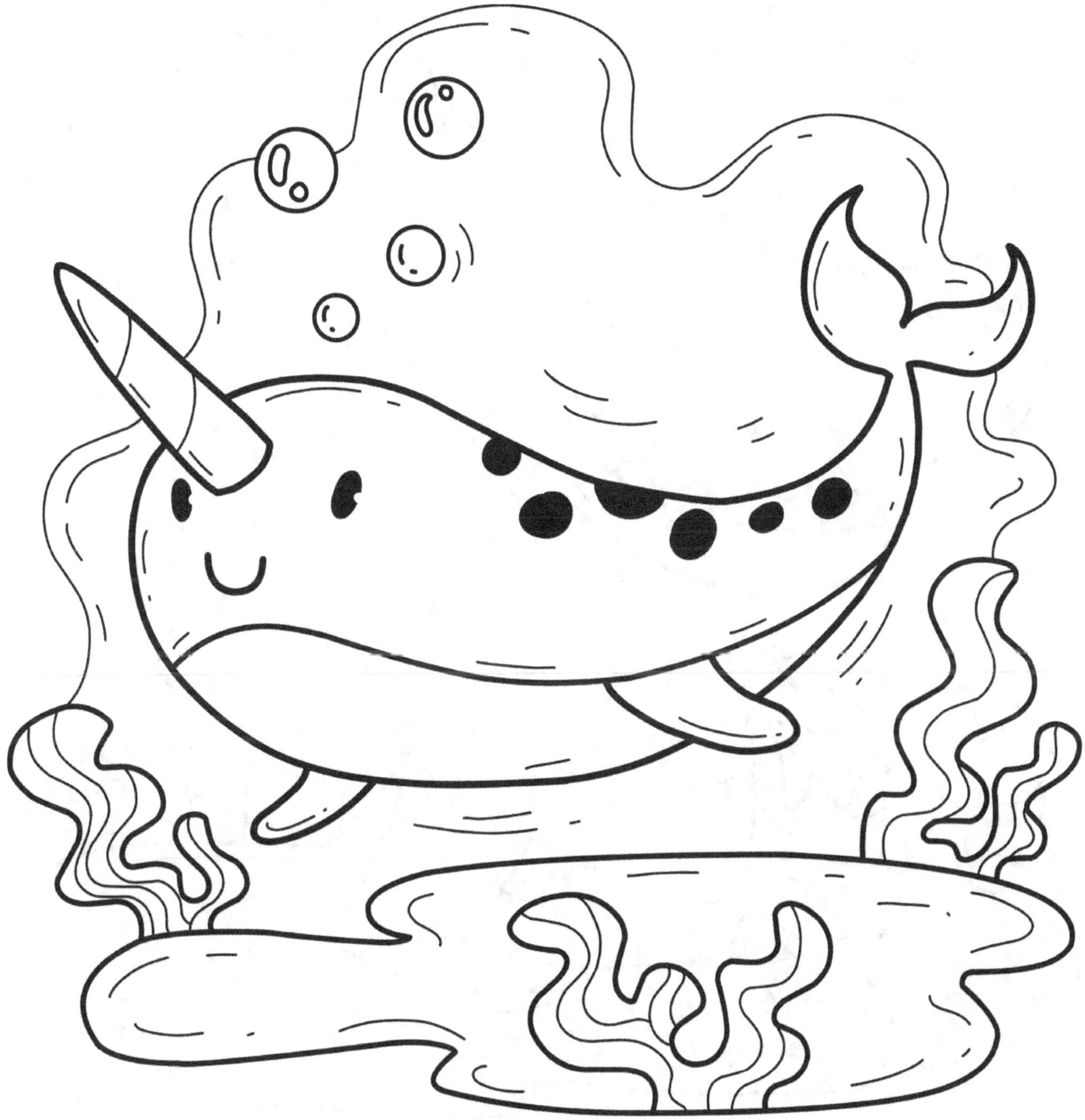

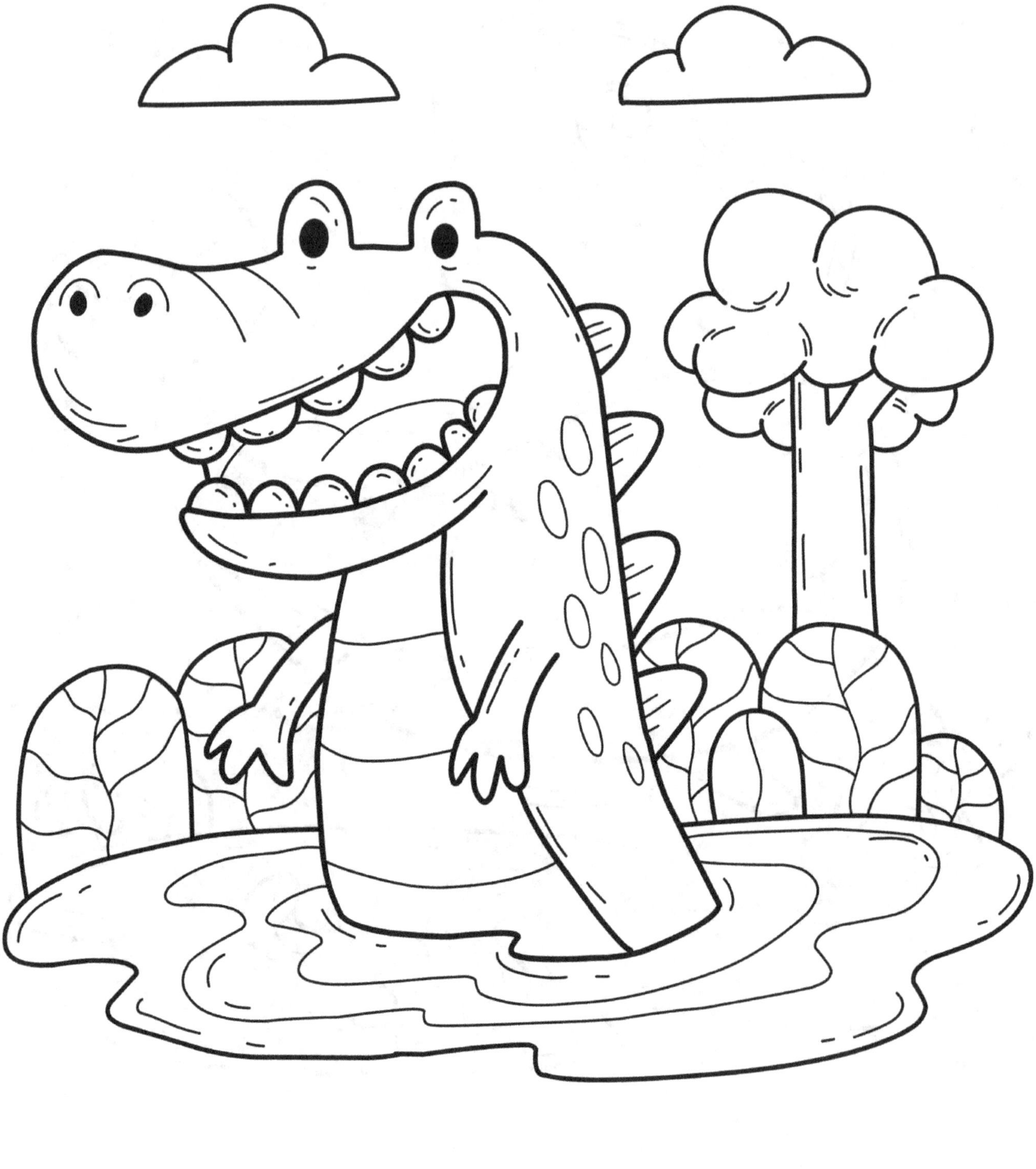

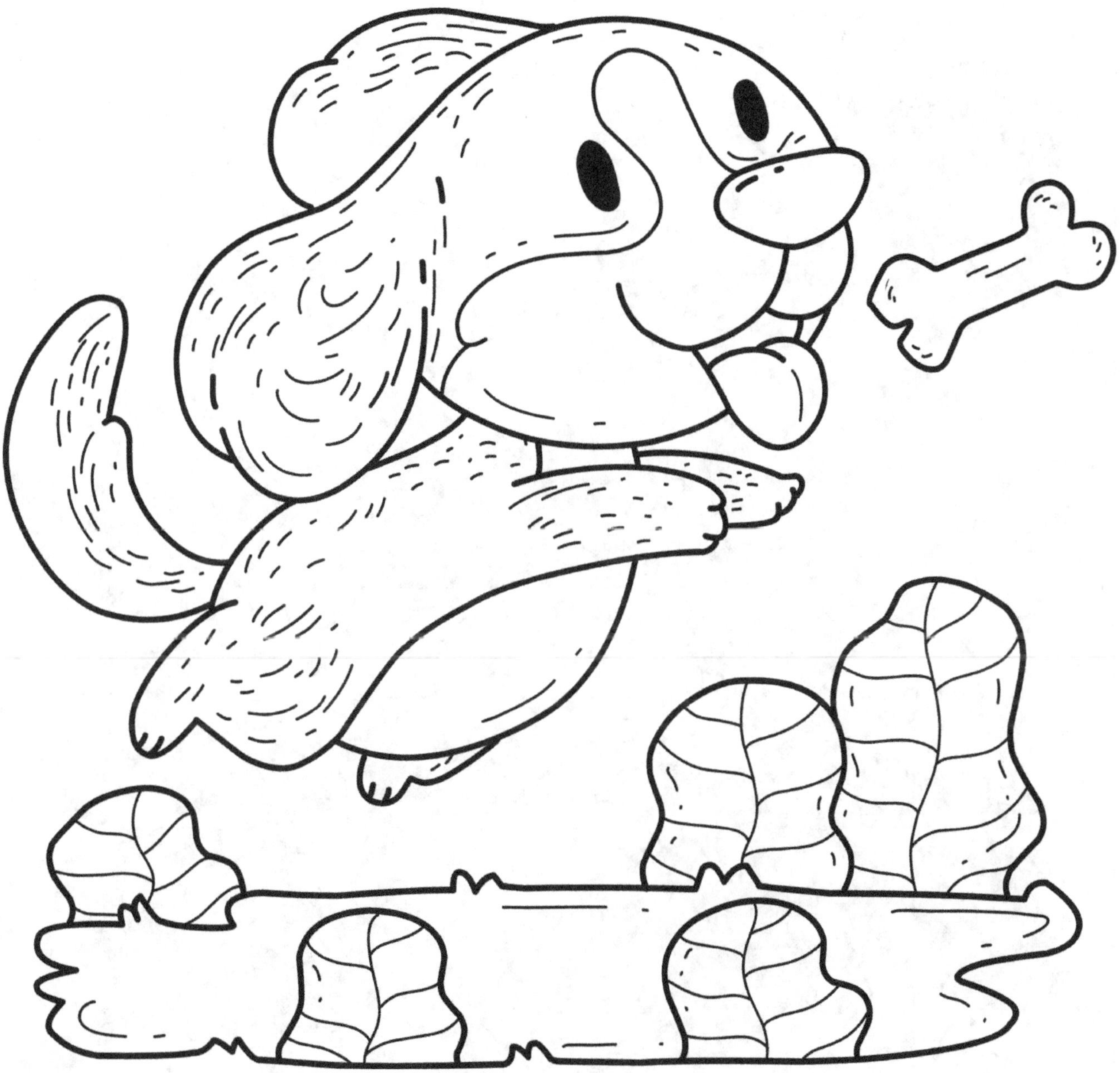

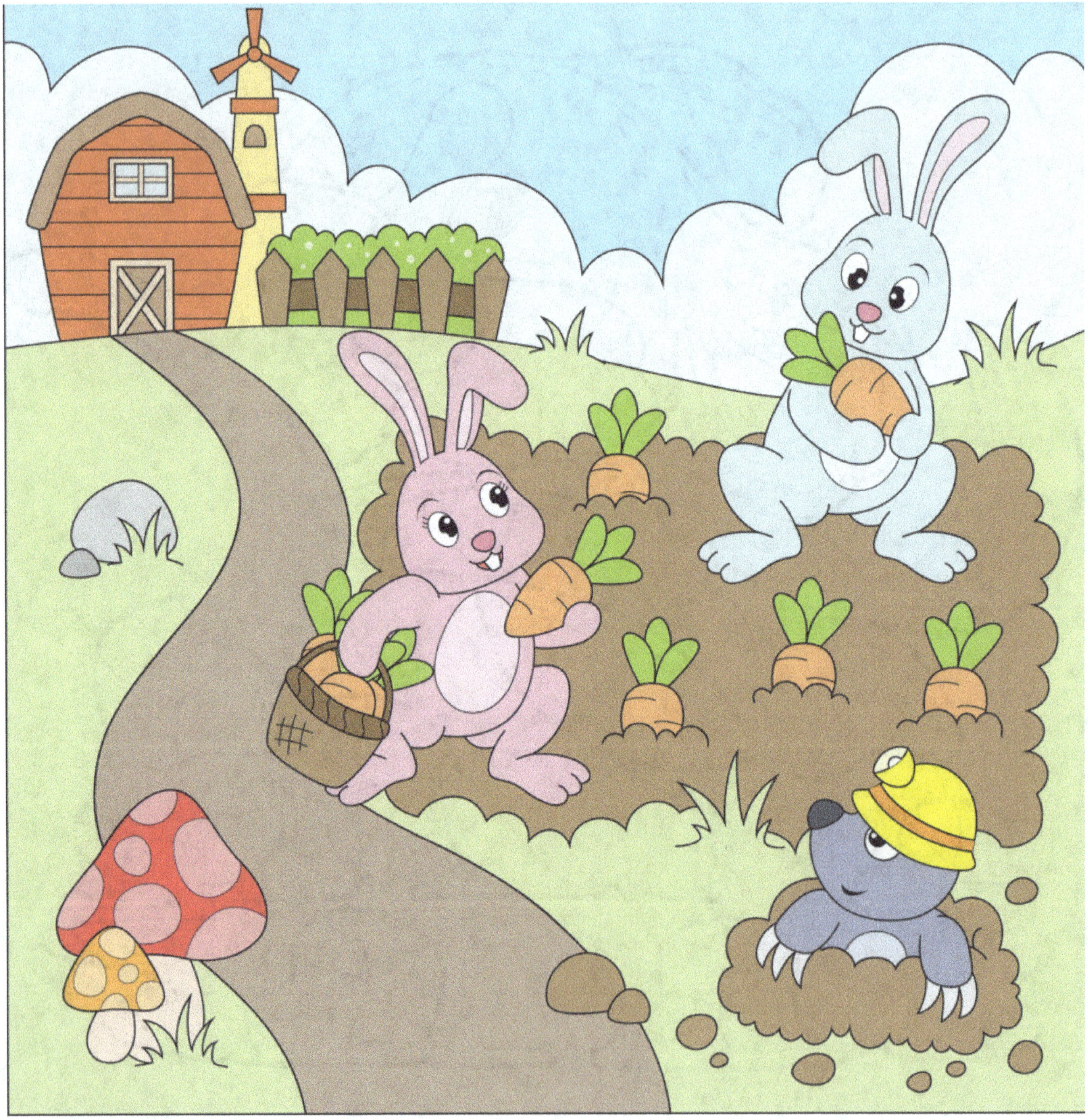

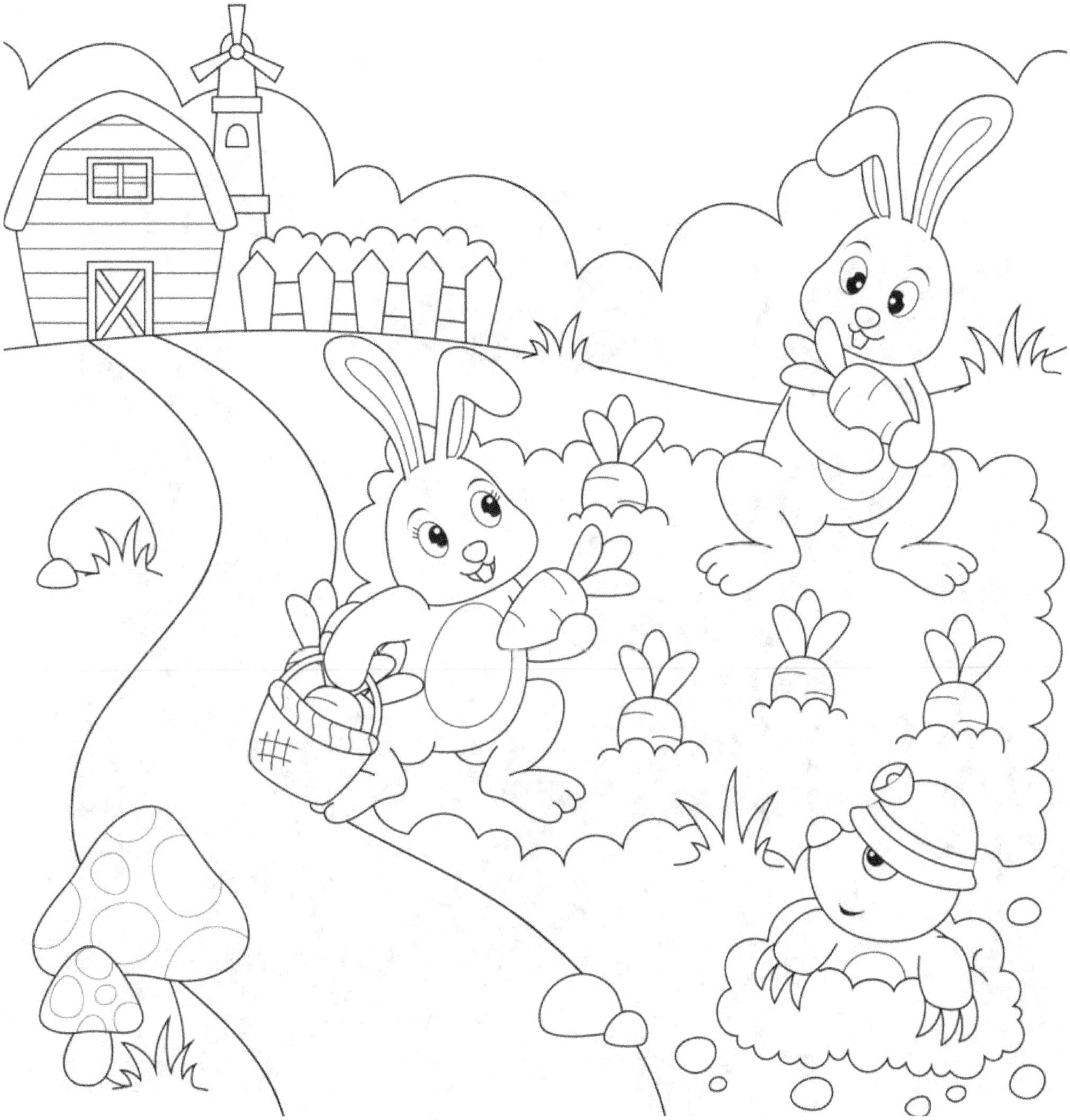

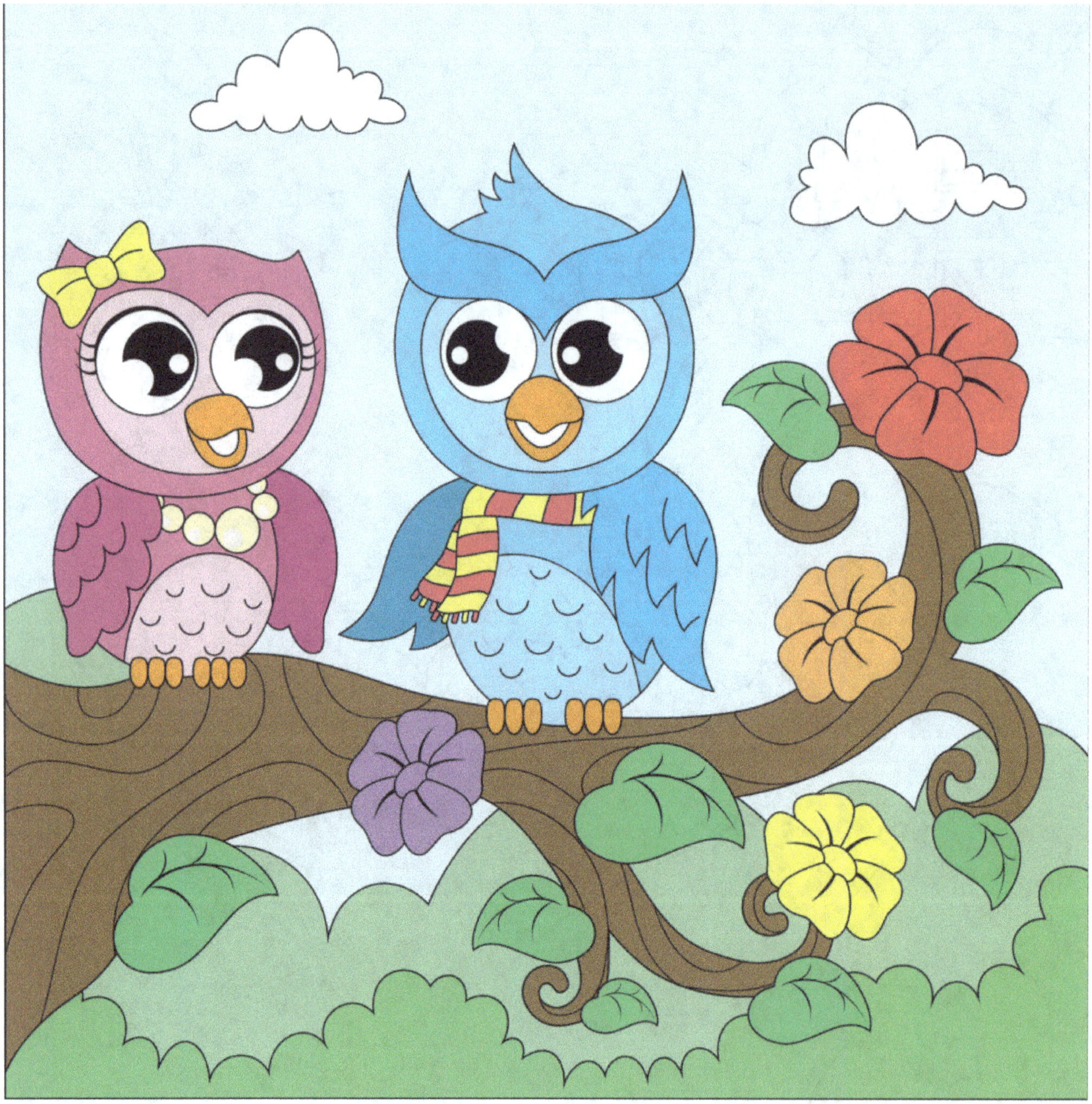

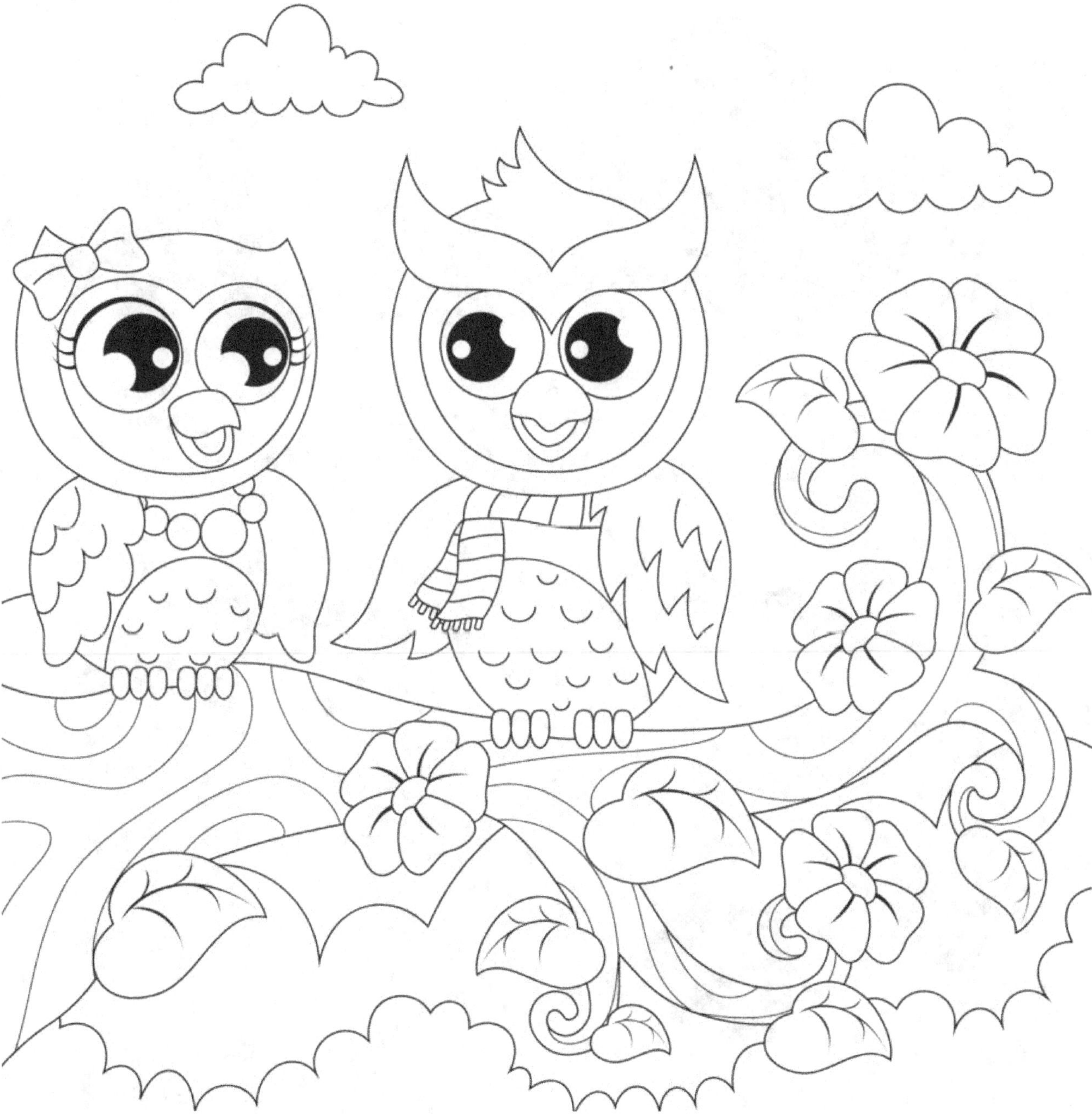

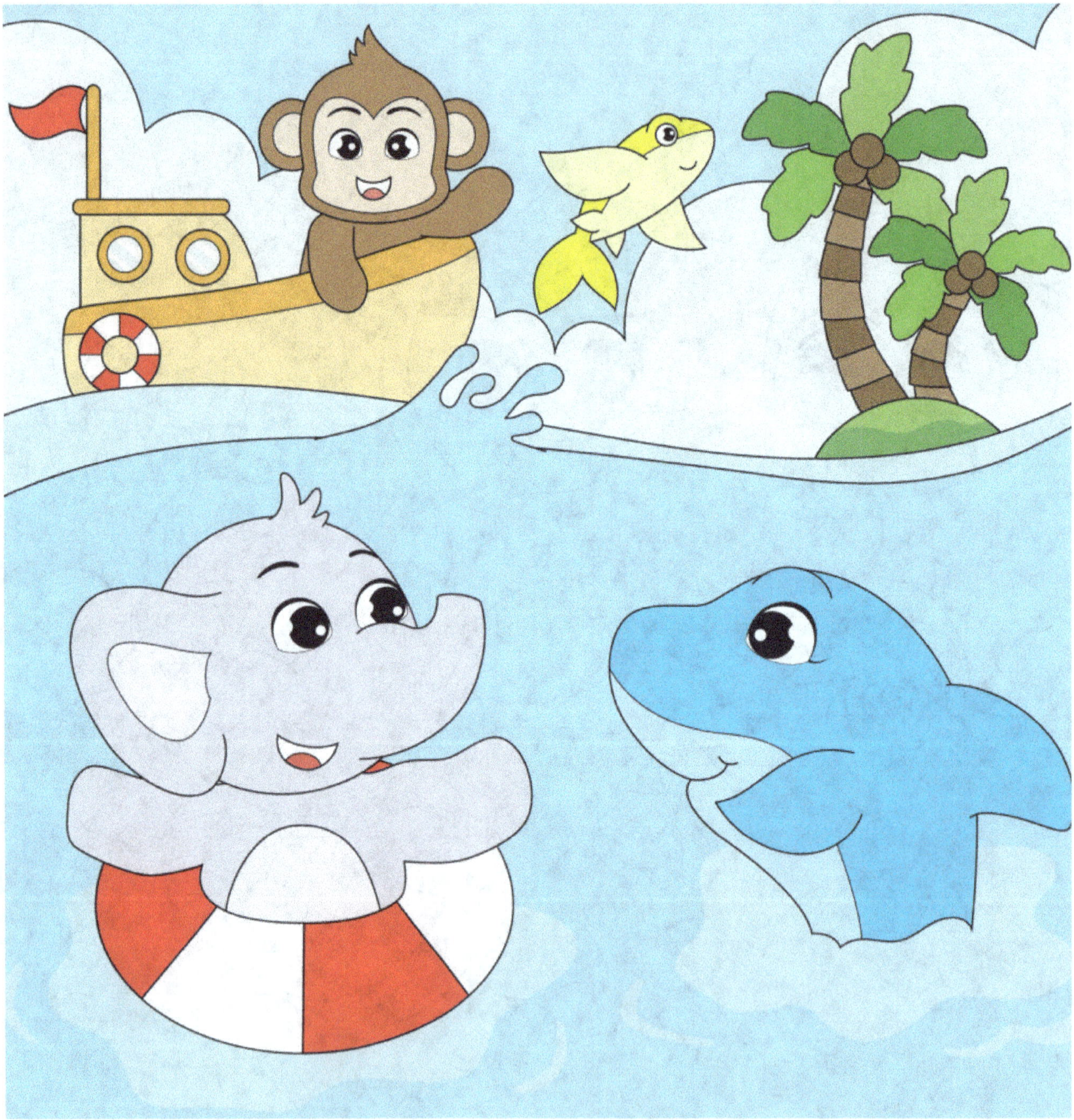

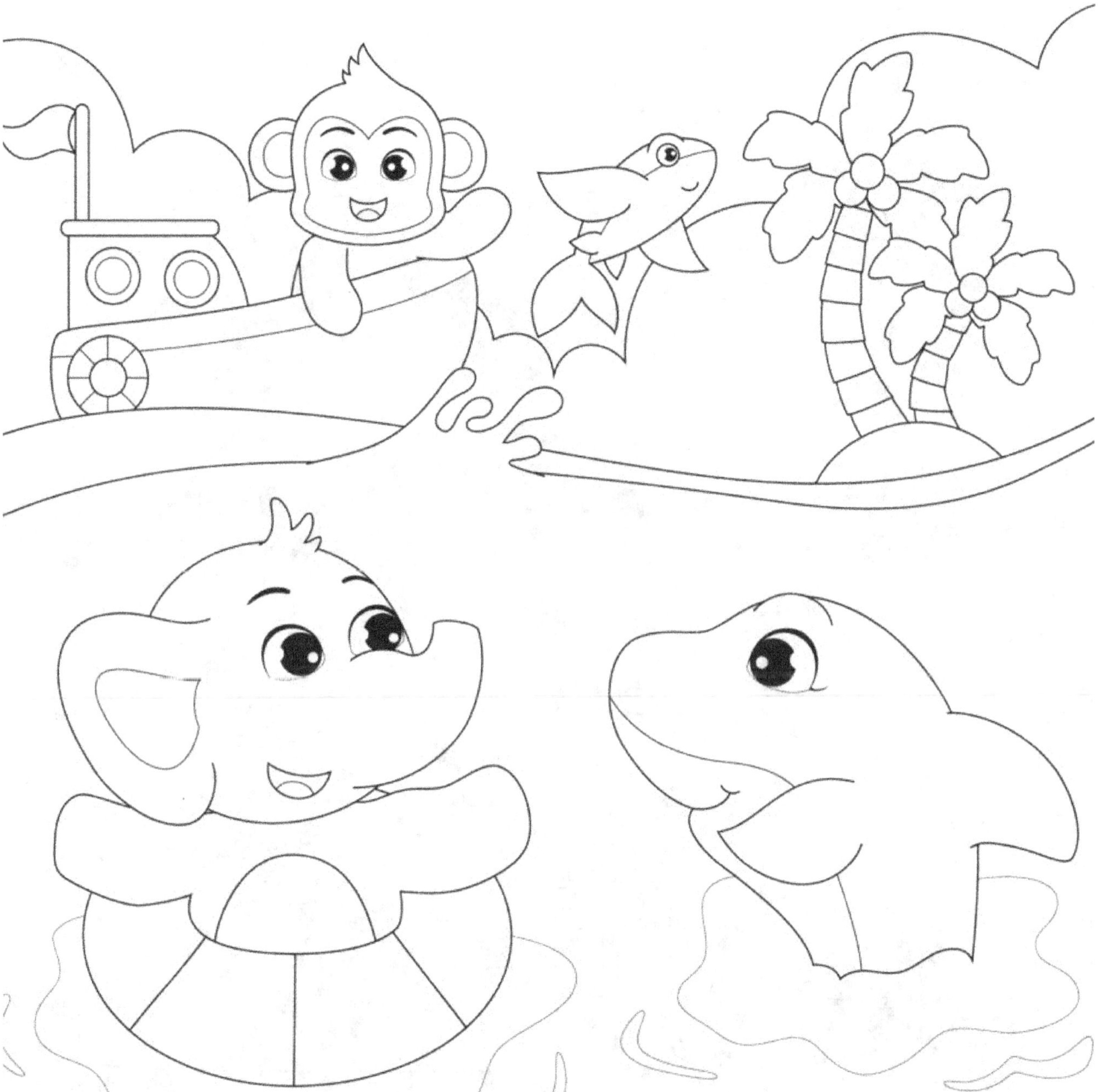

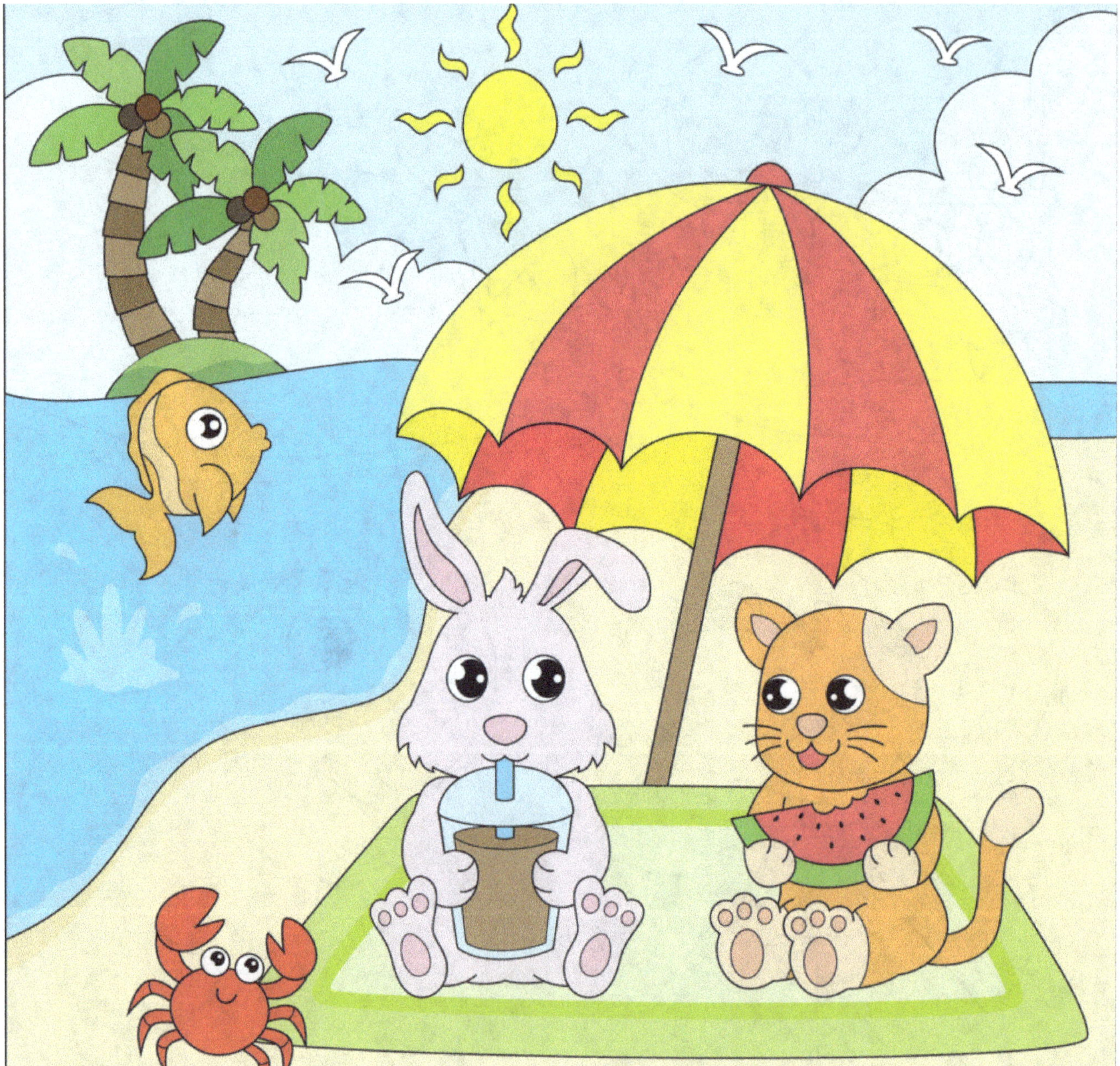

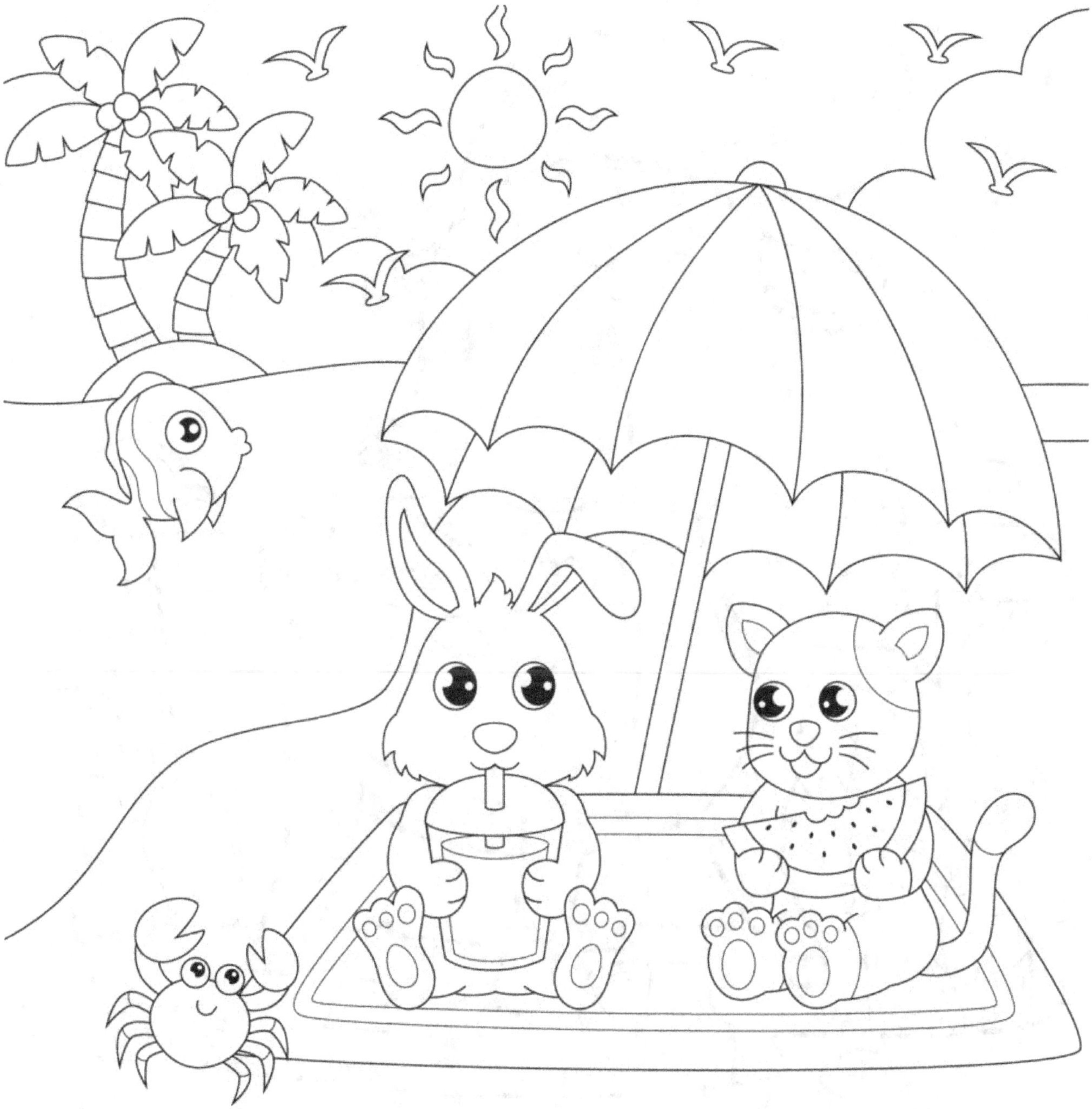

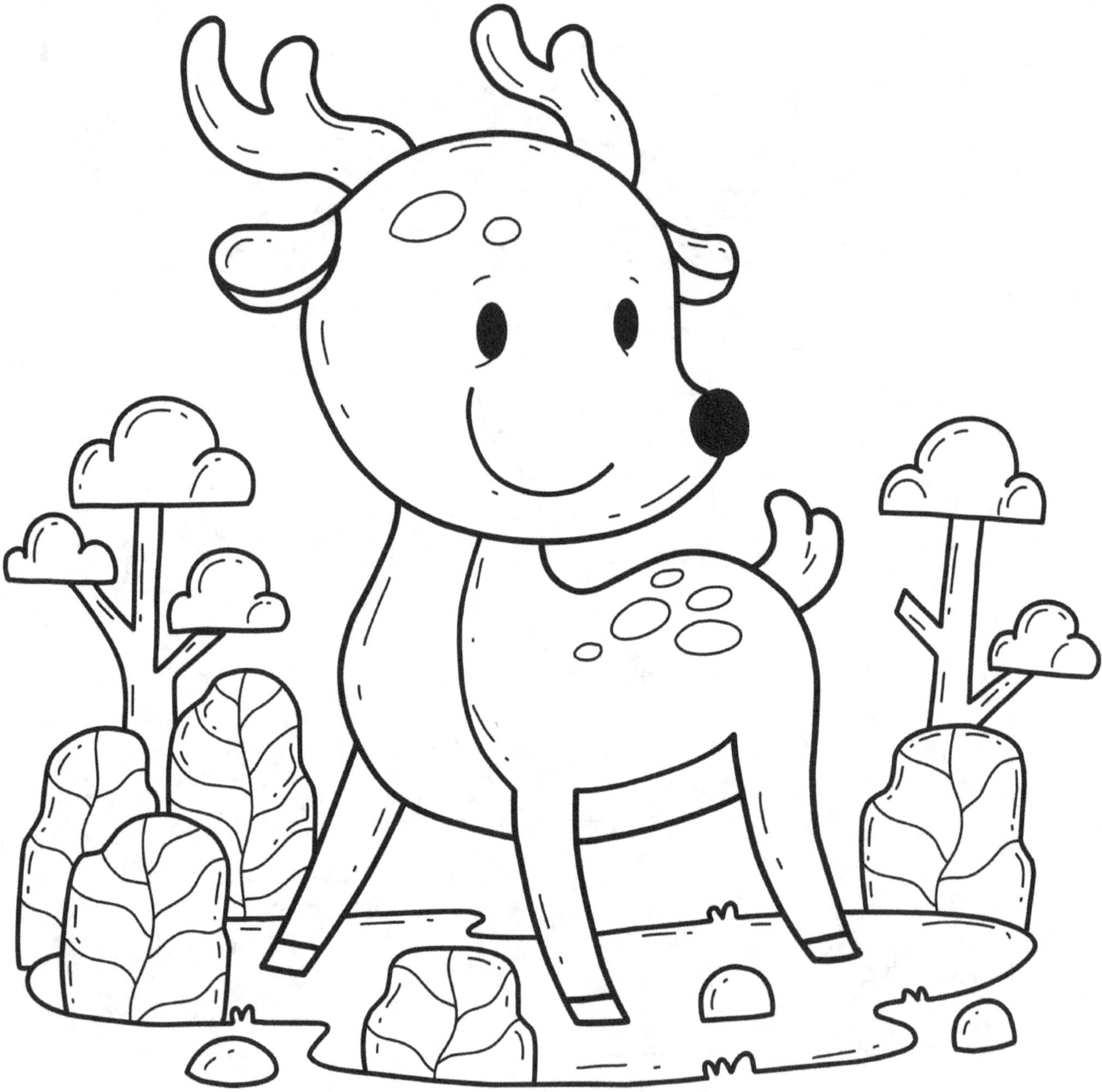

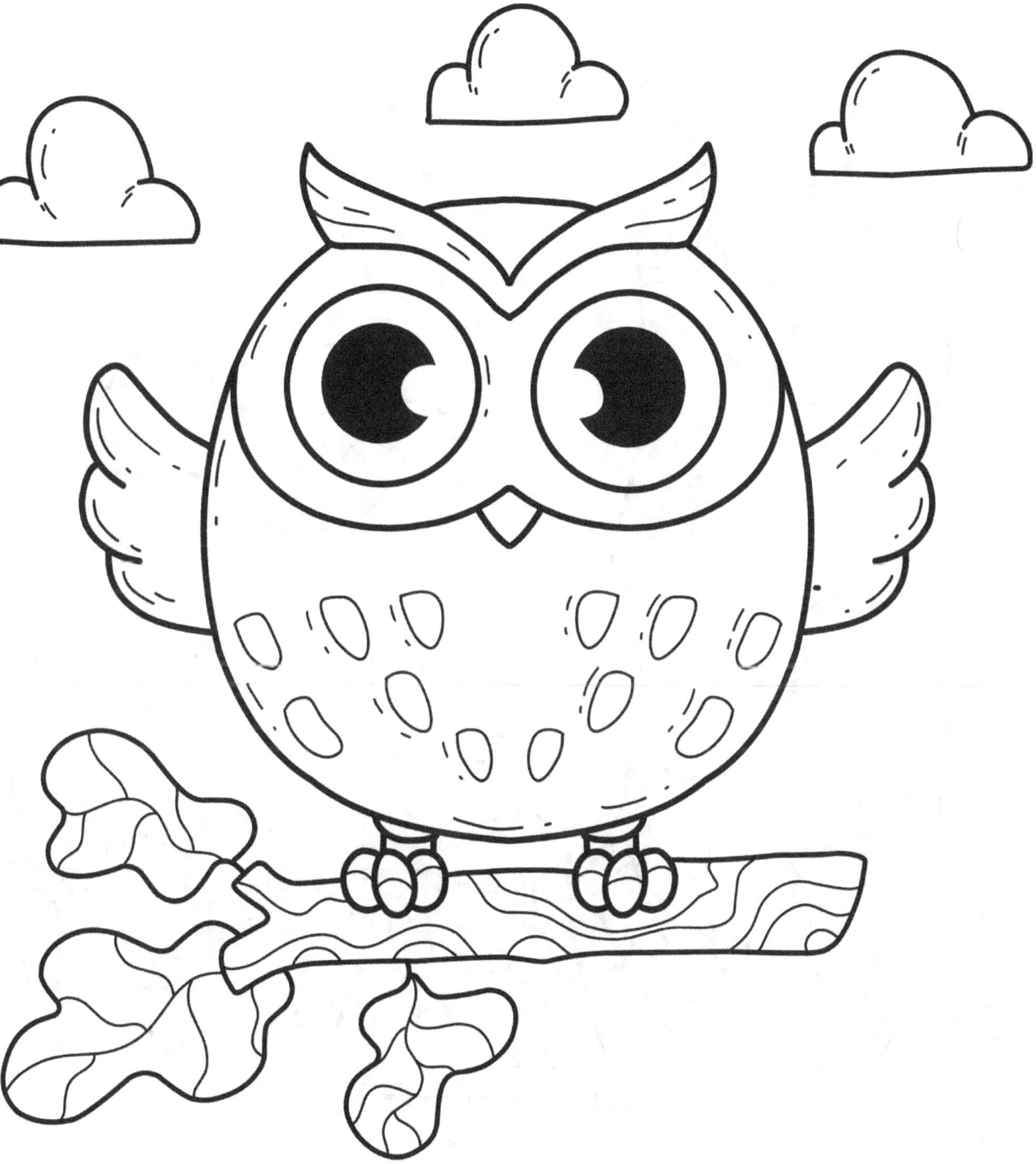

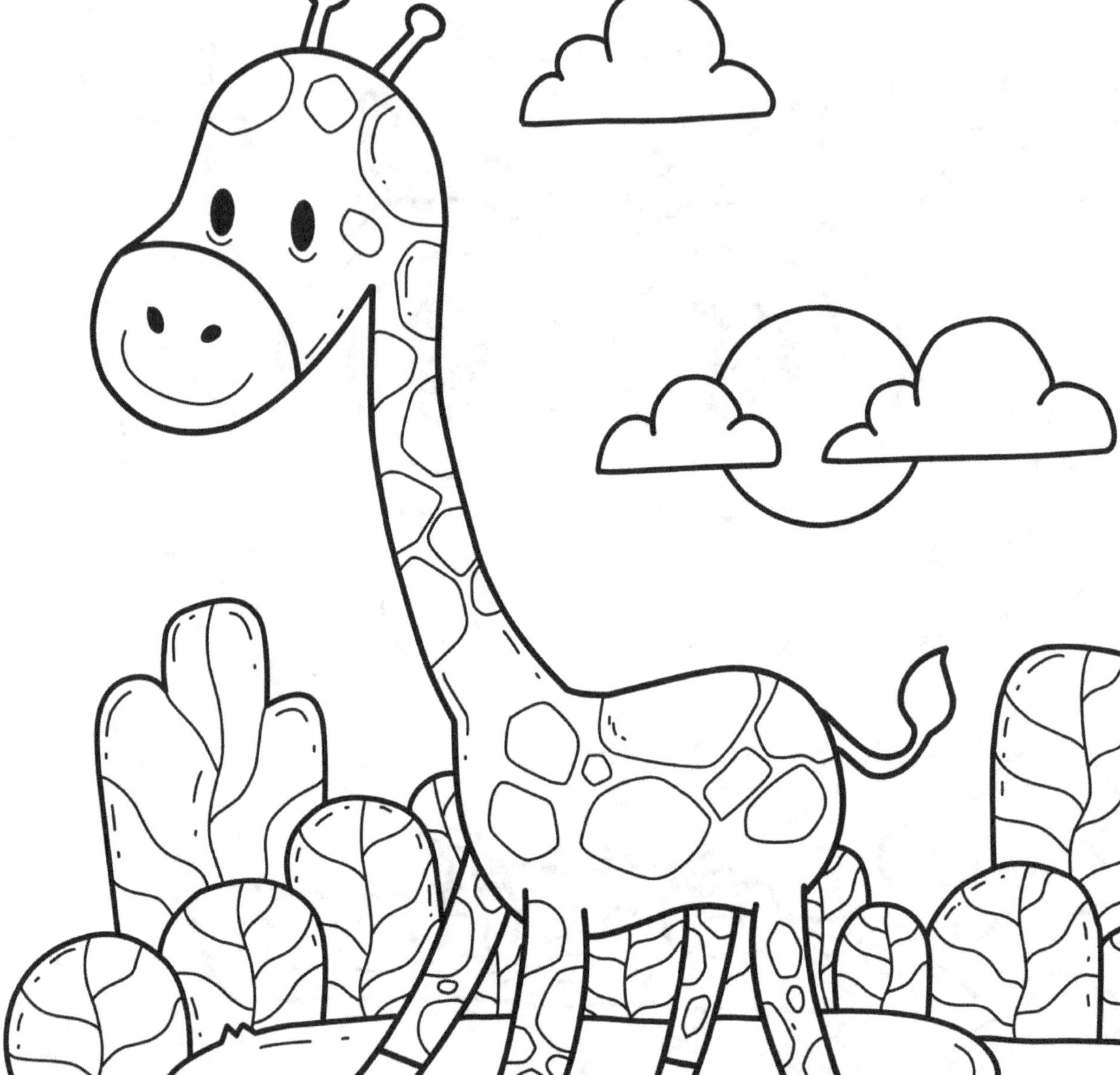

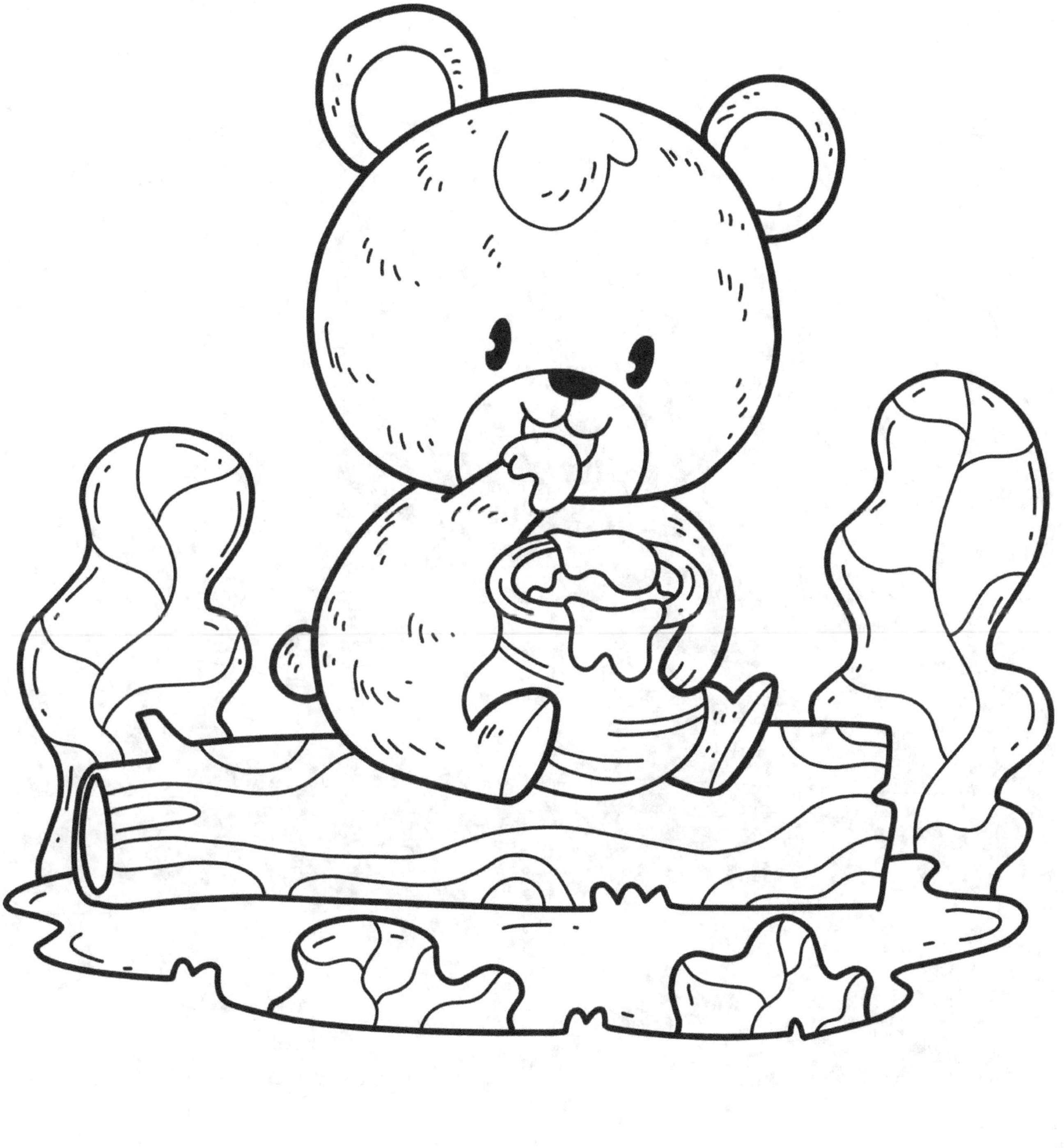

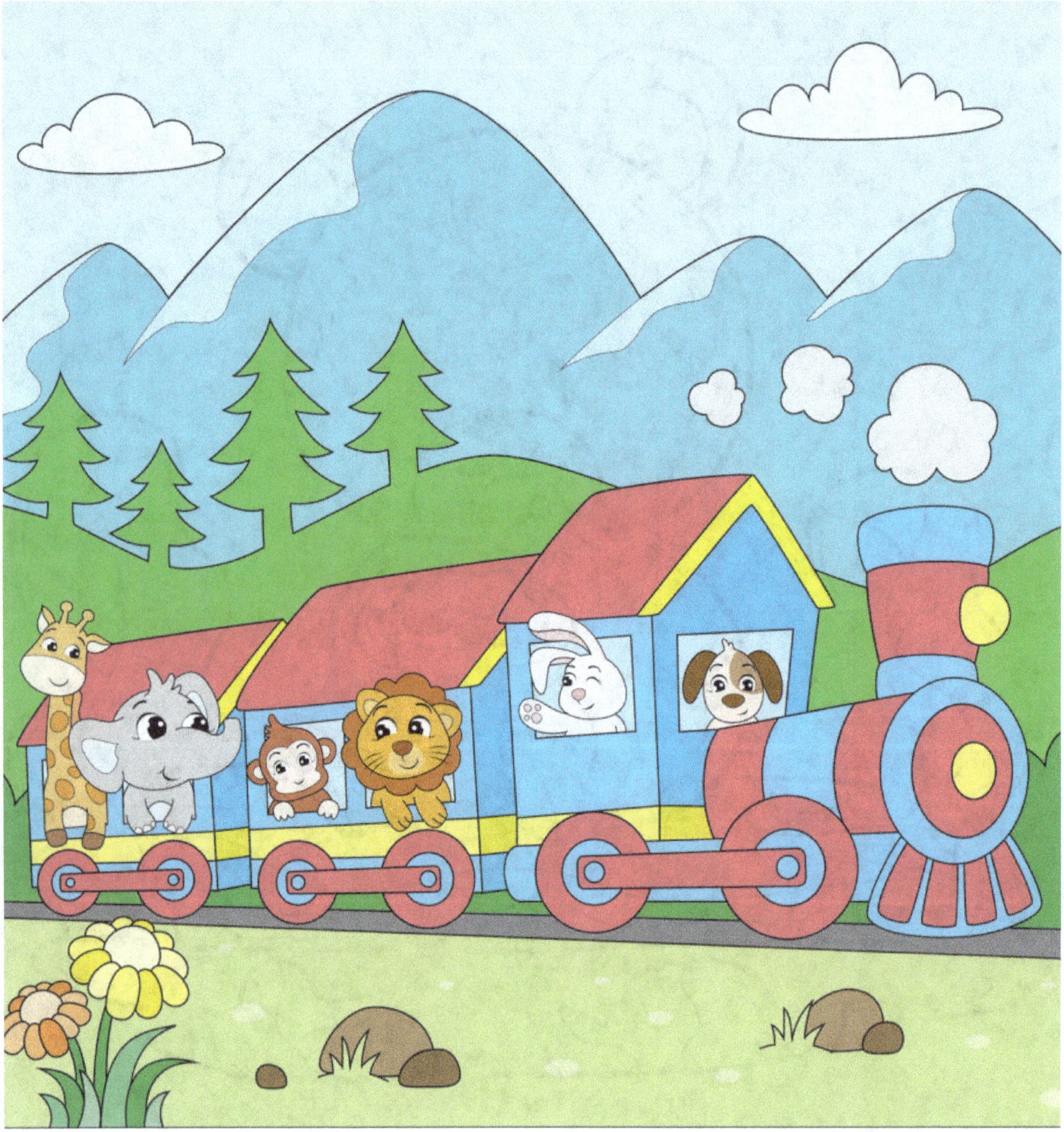

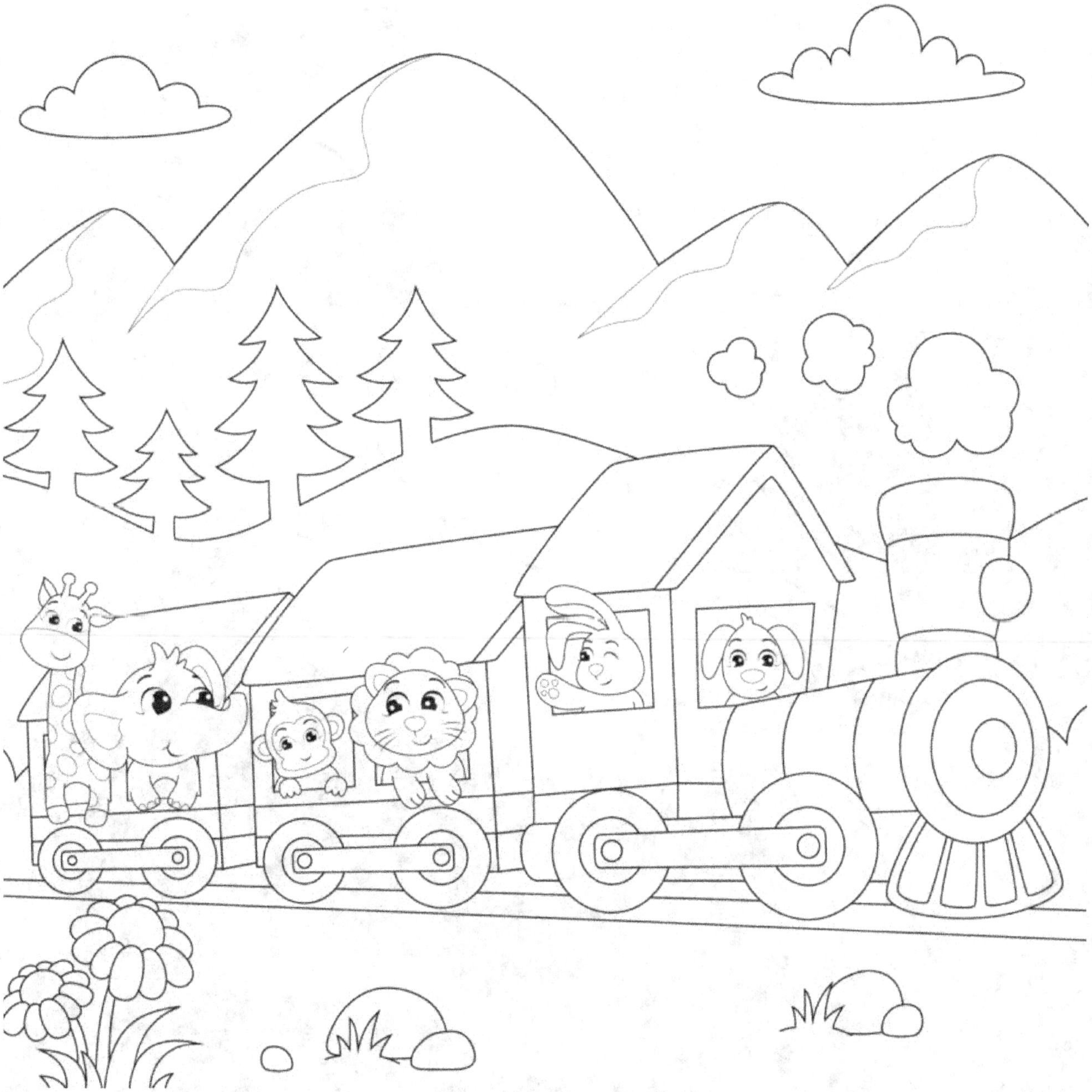

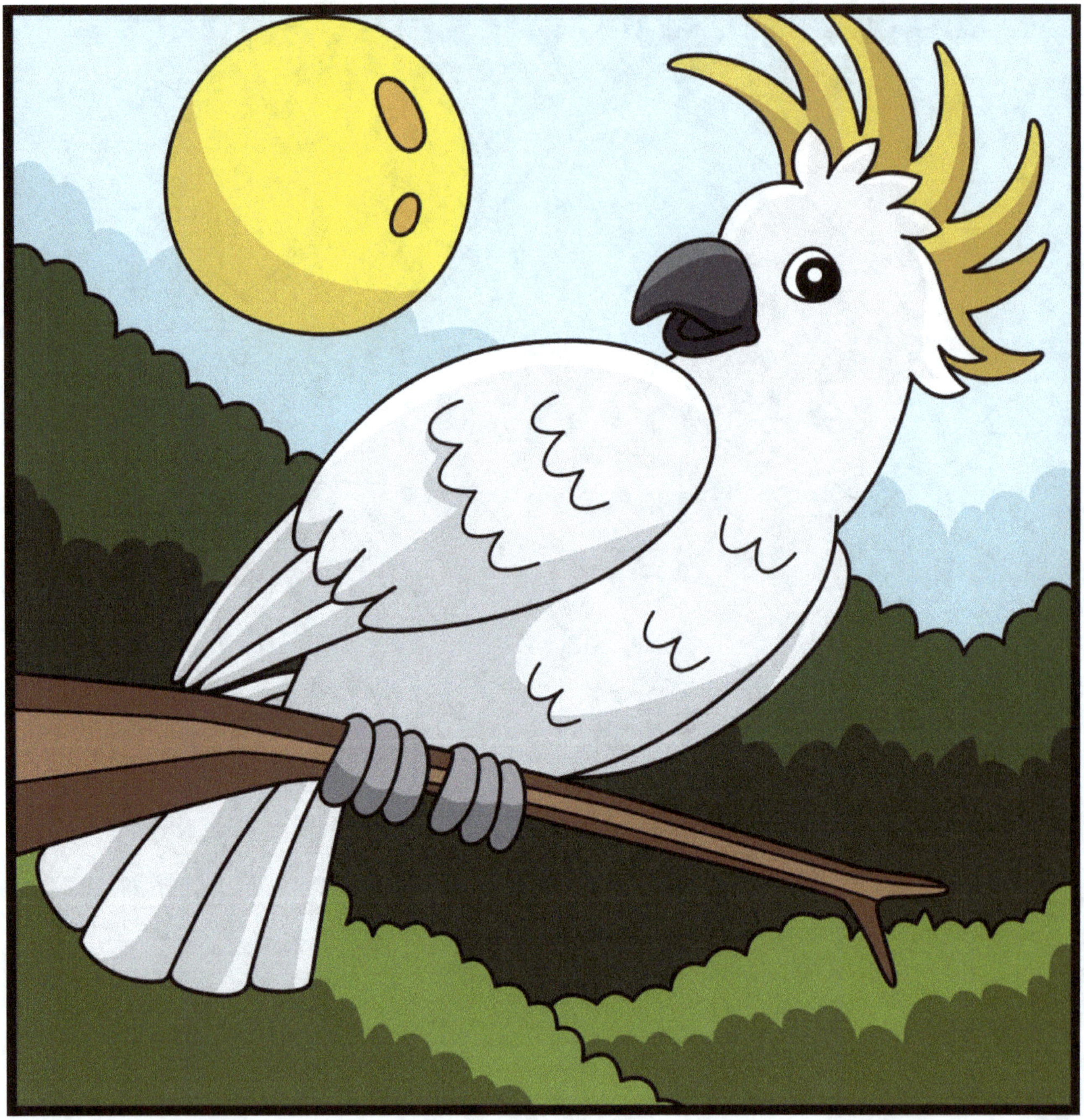

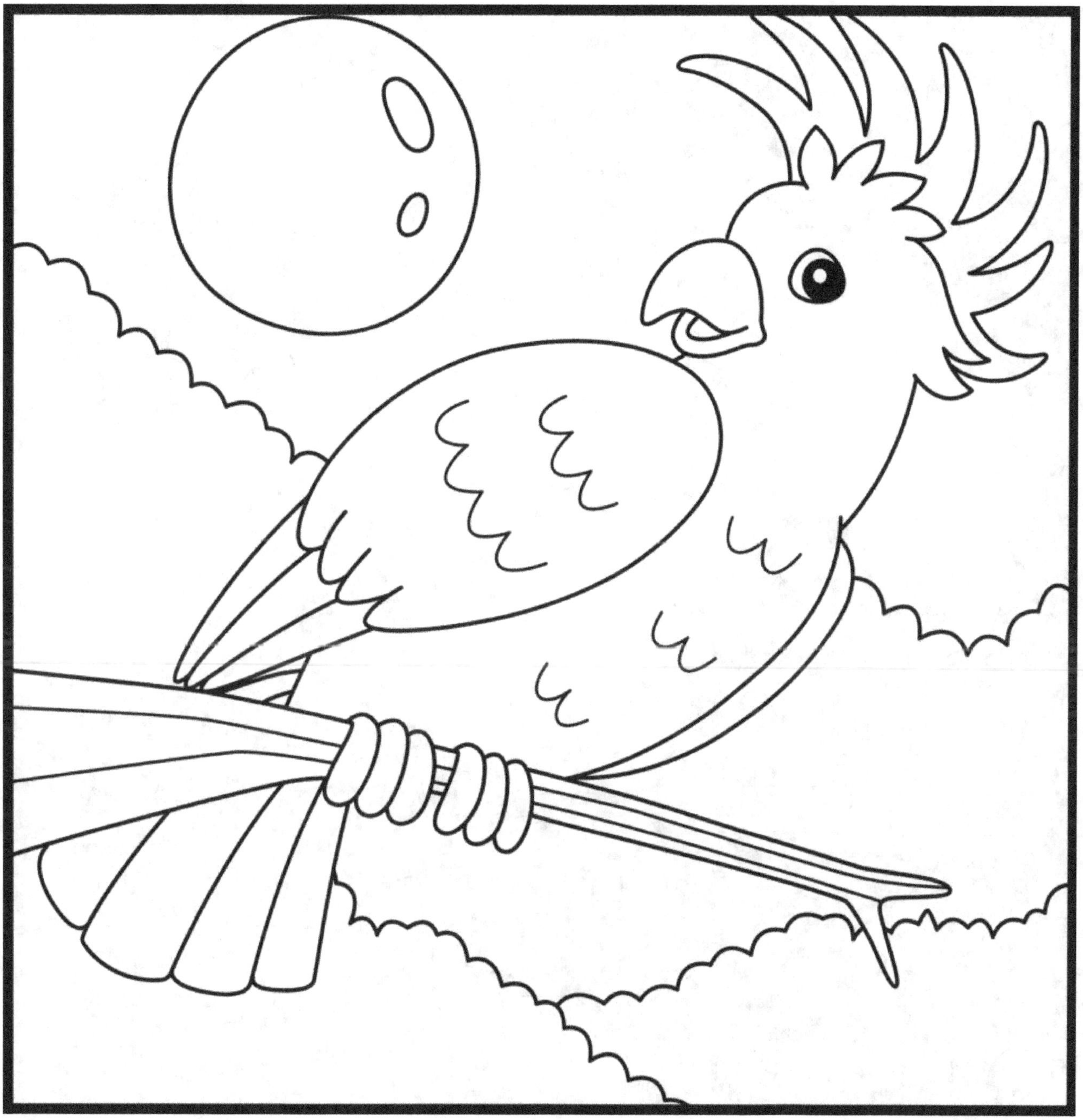

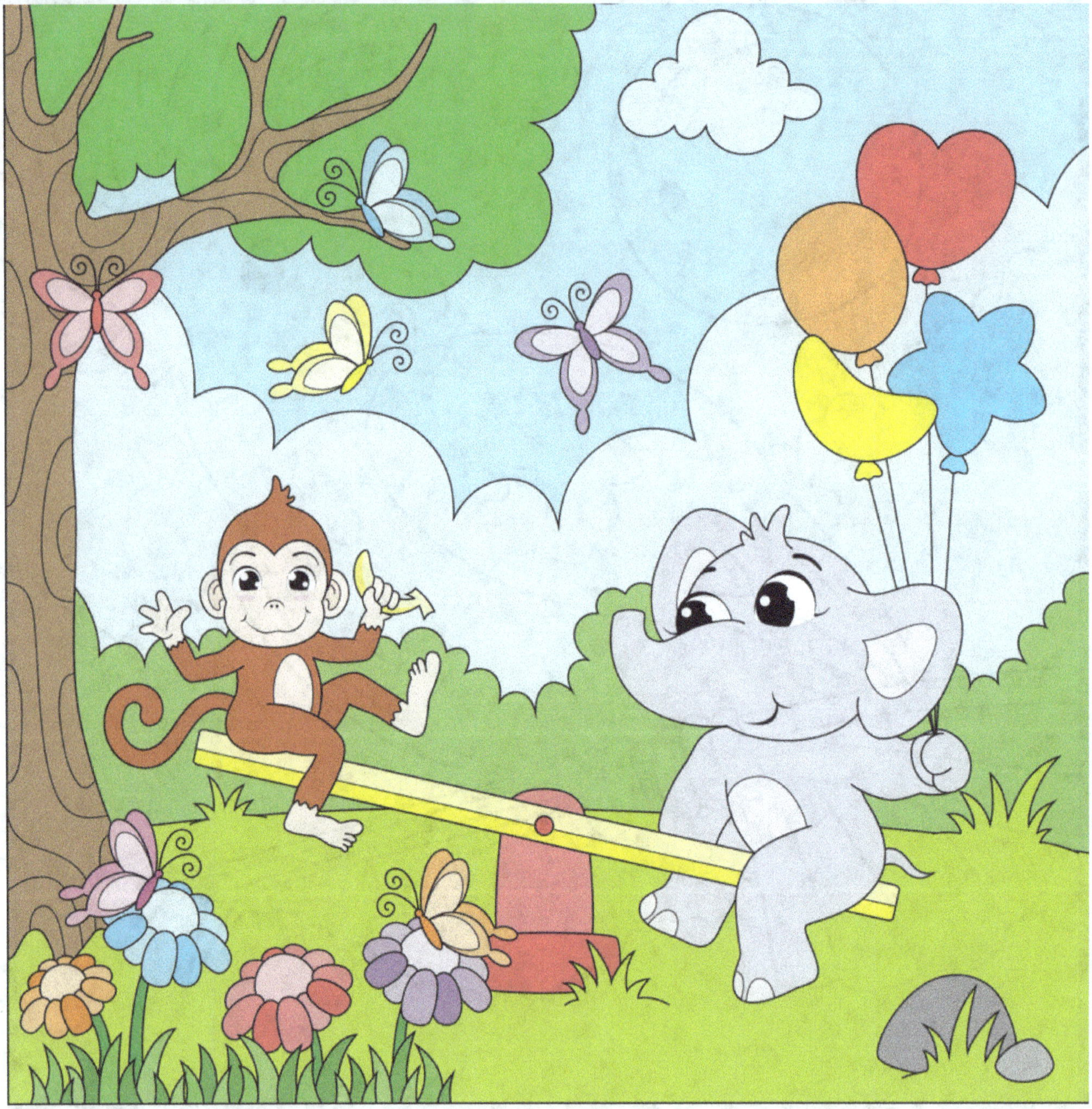

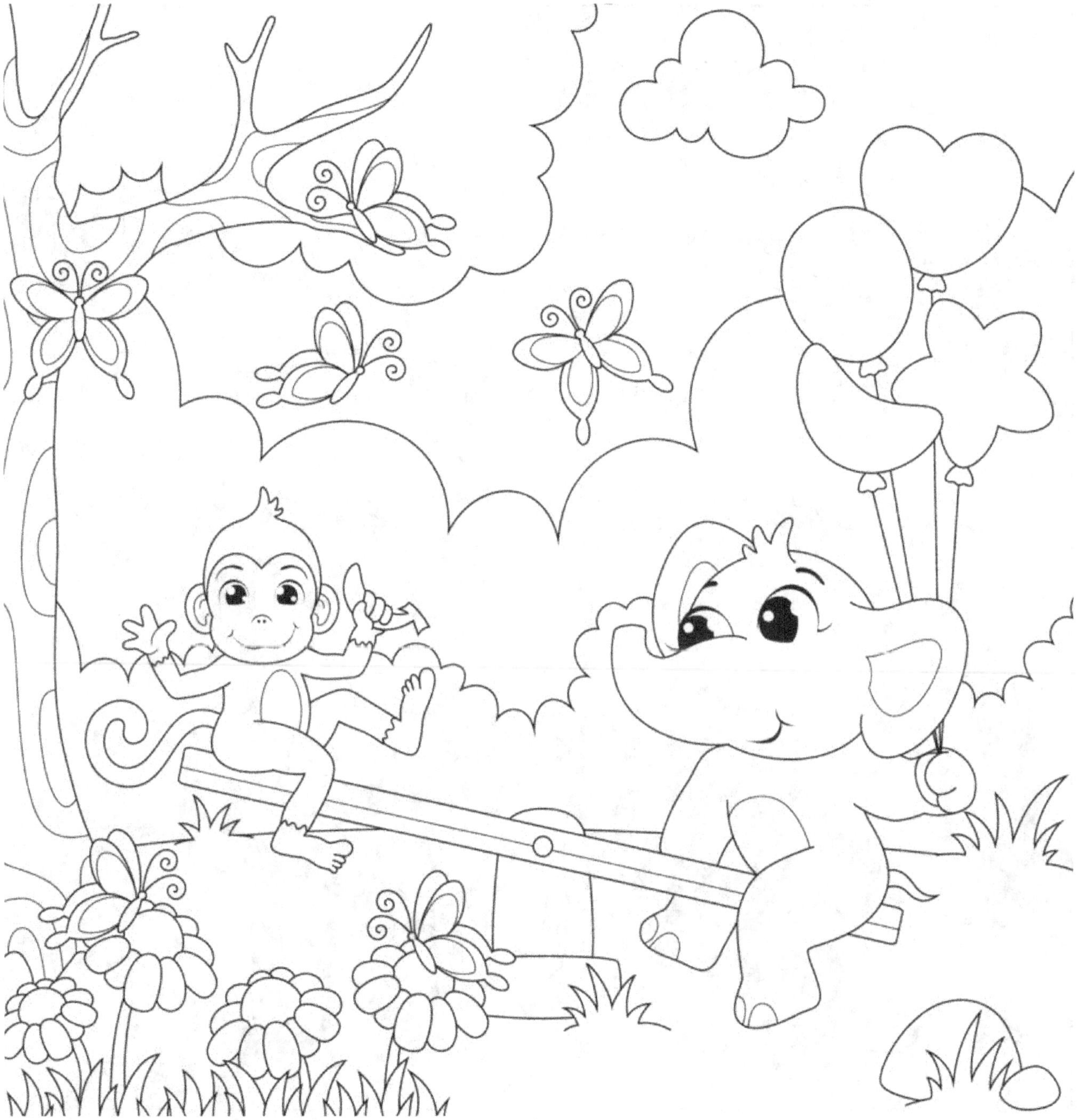

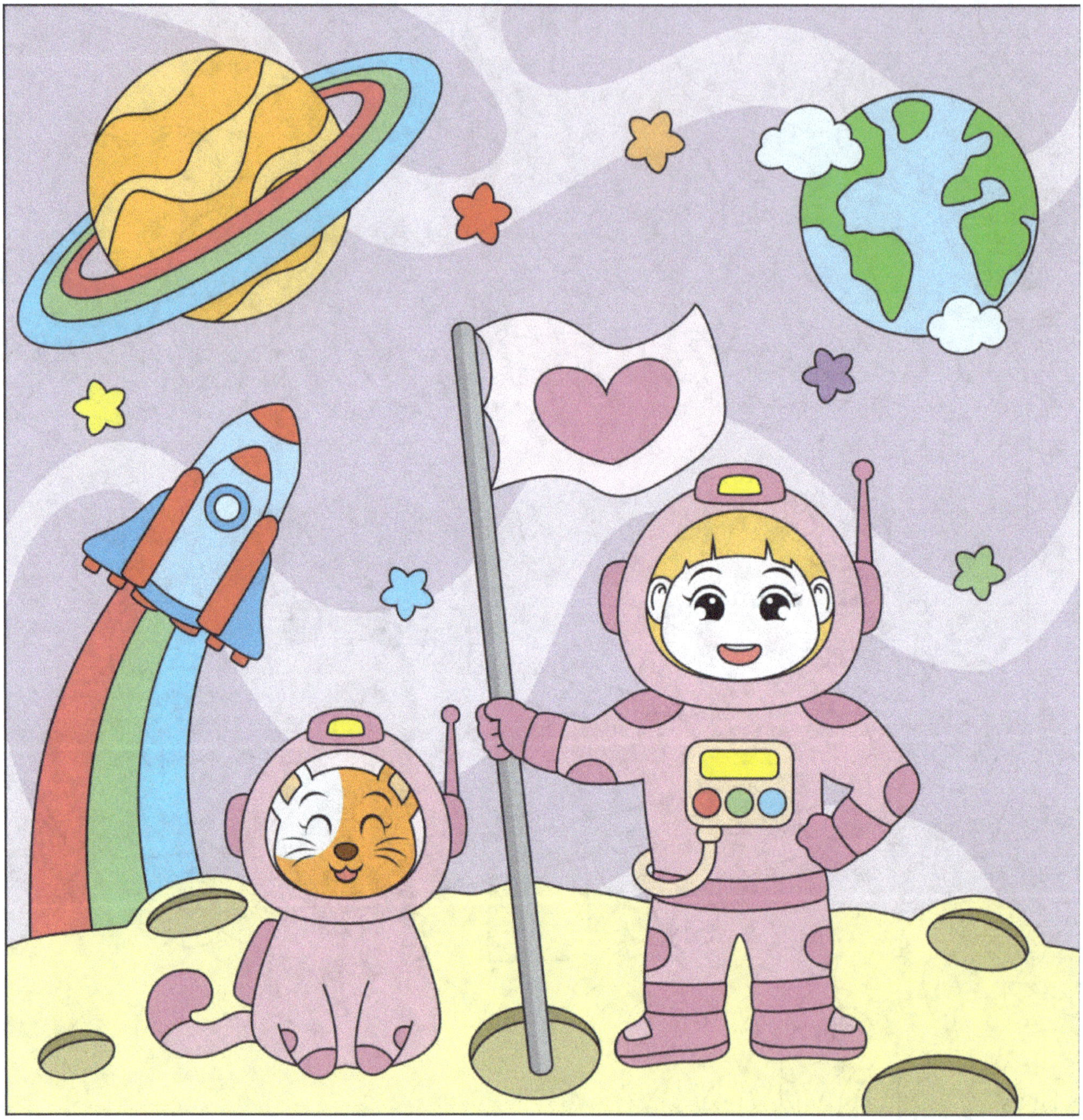

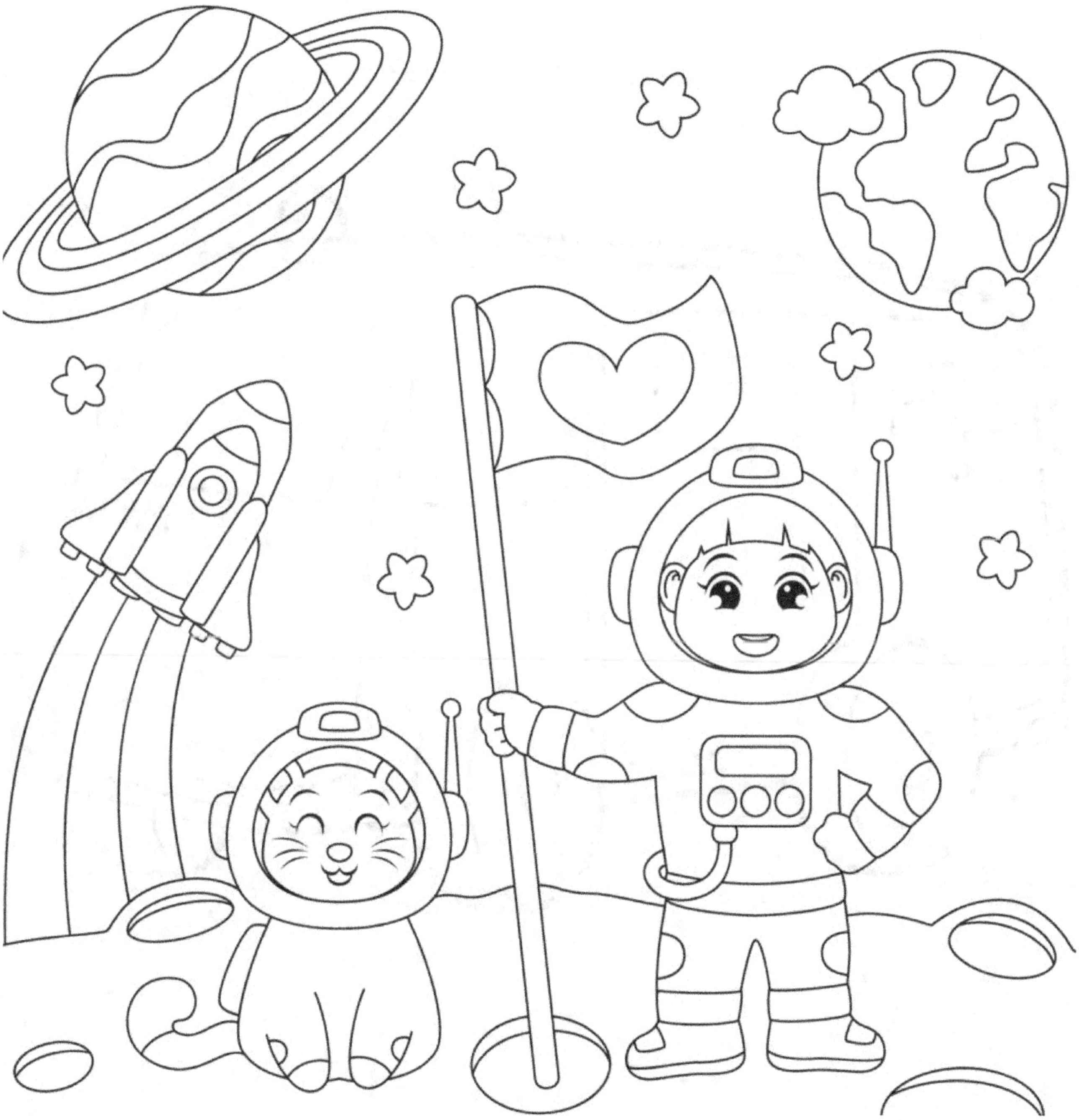

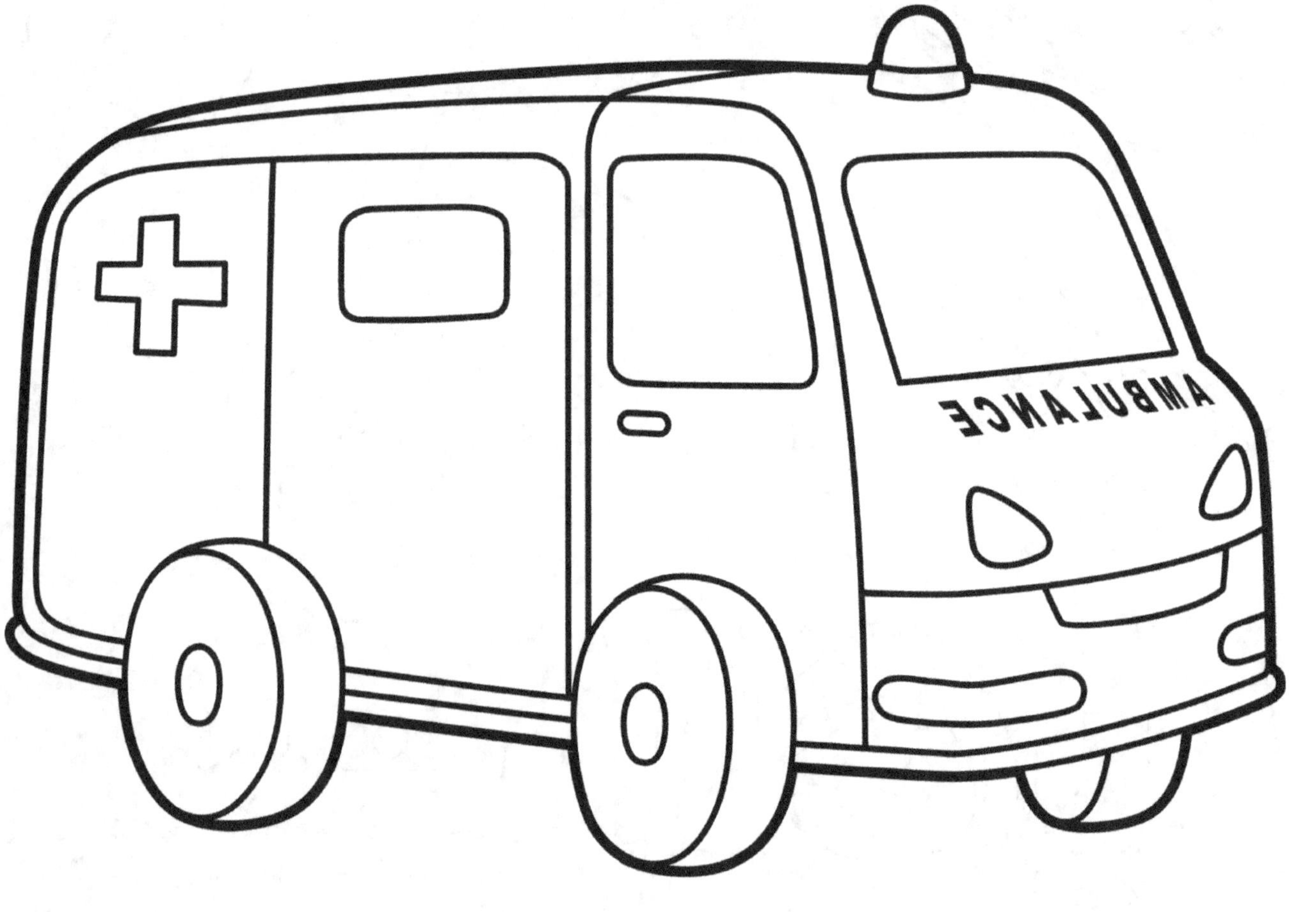
AMBULANCE

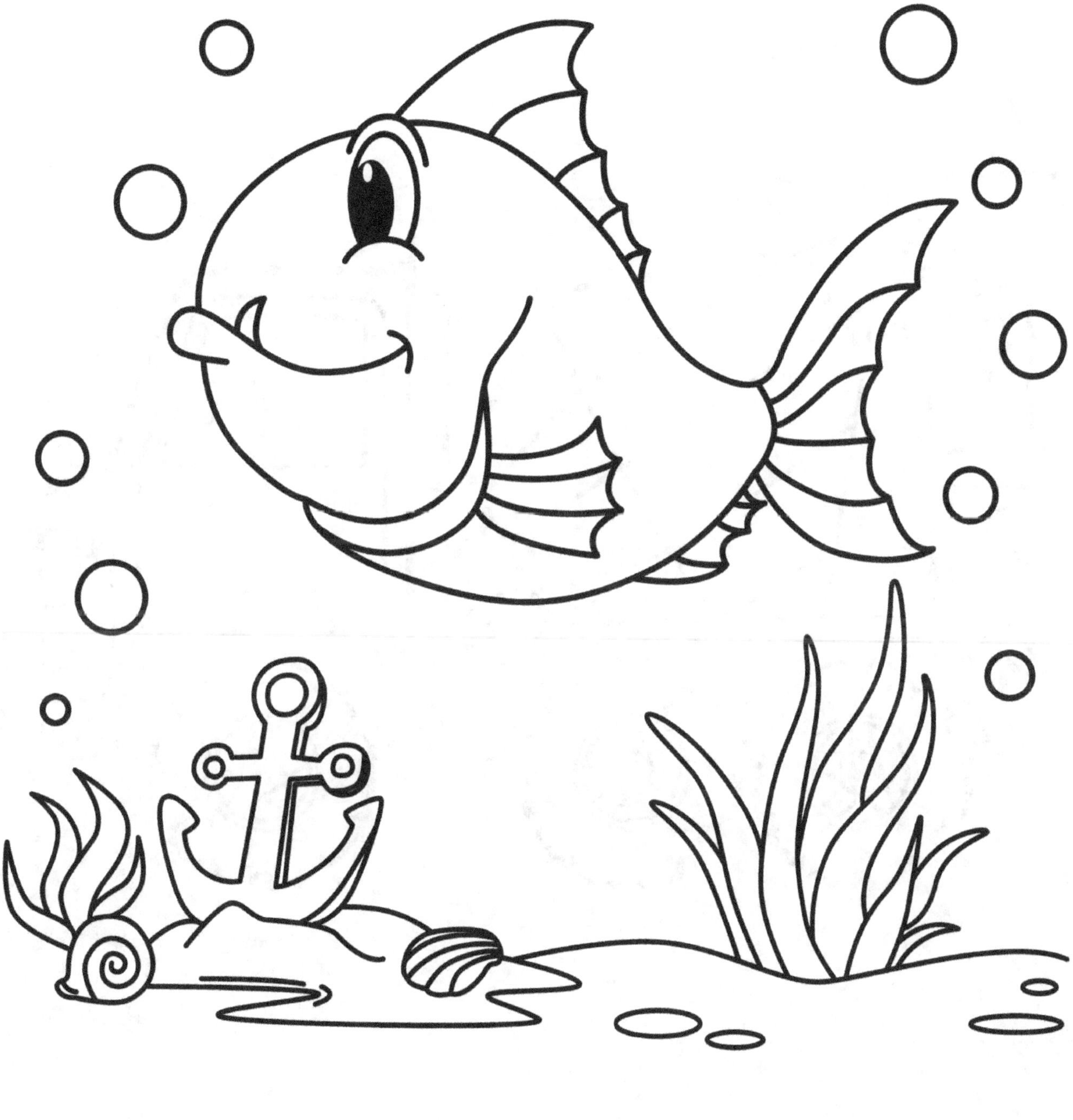

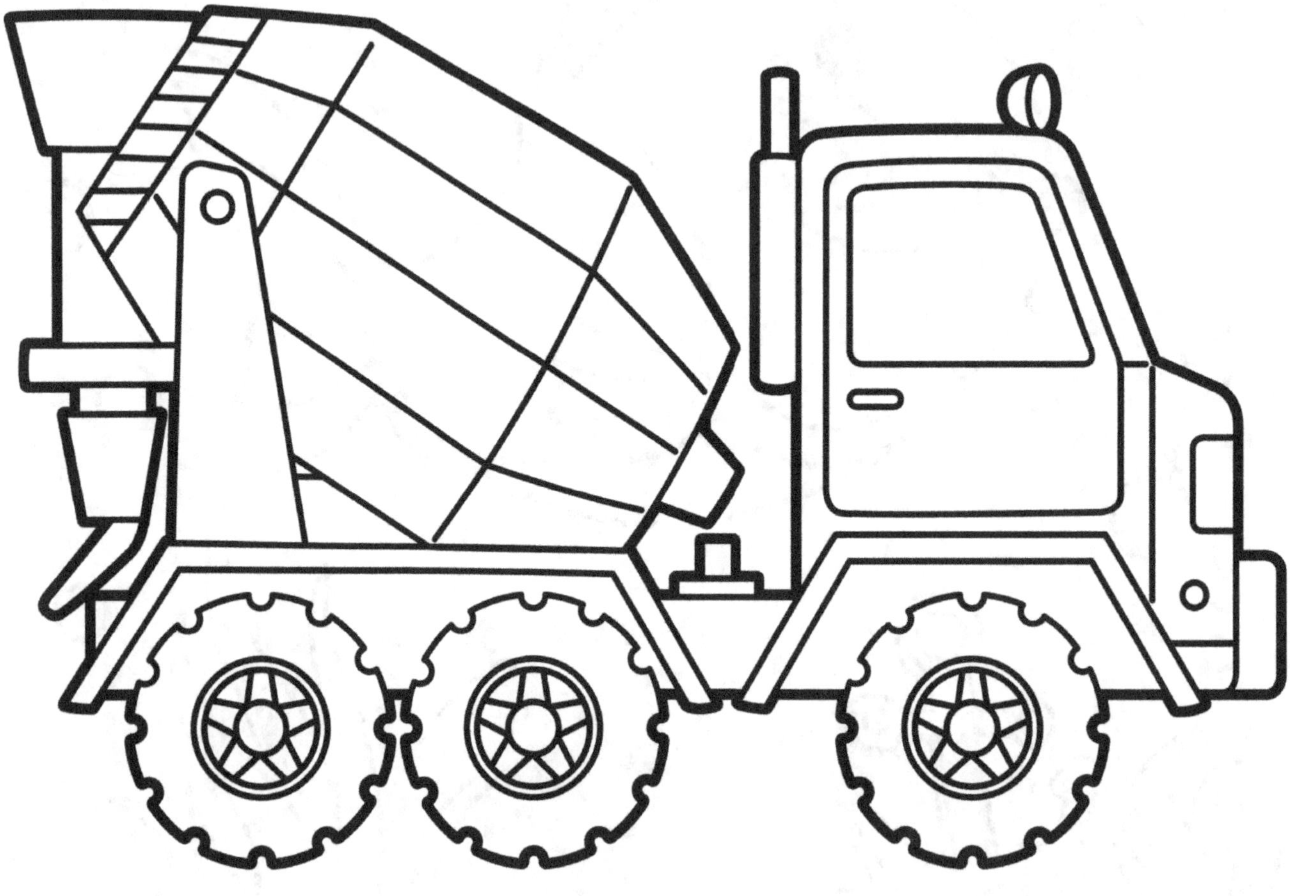

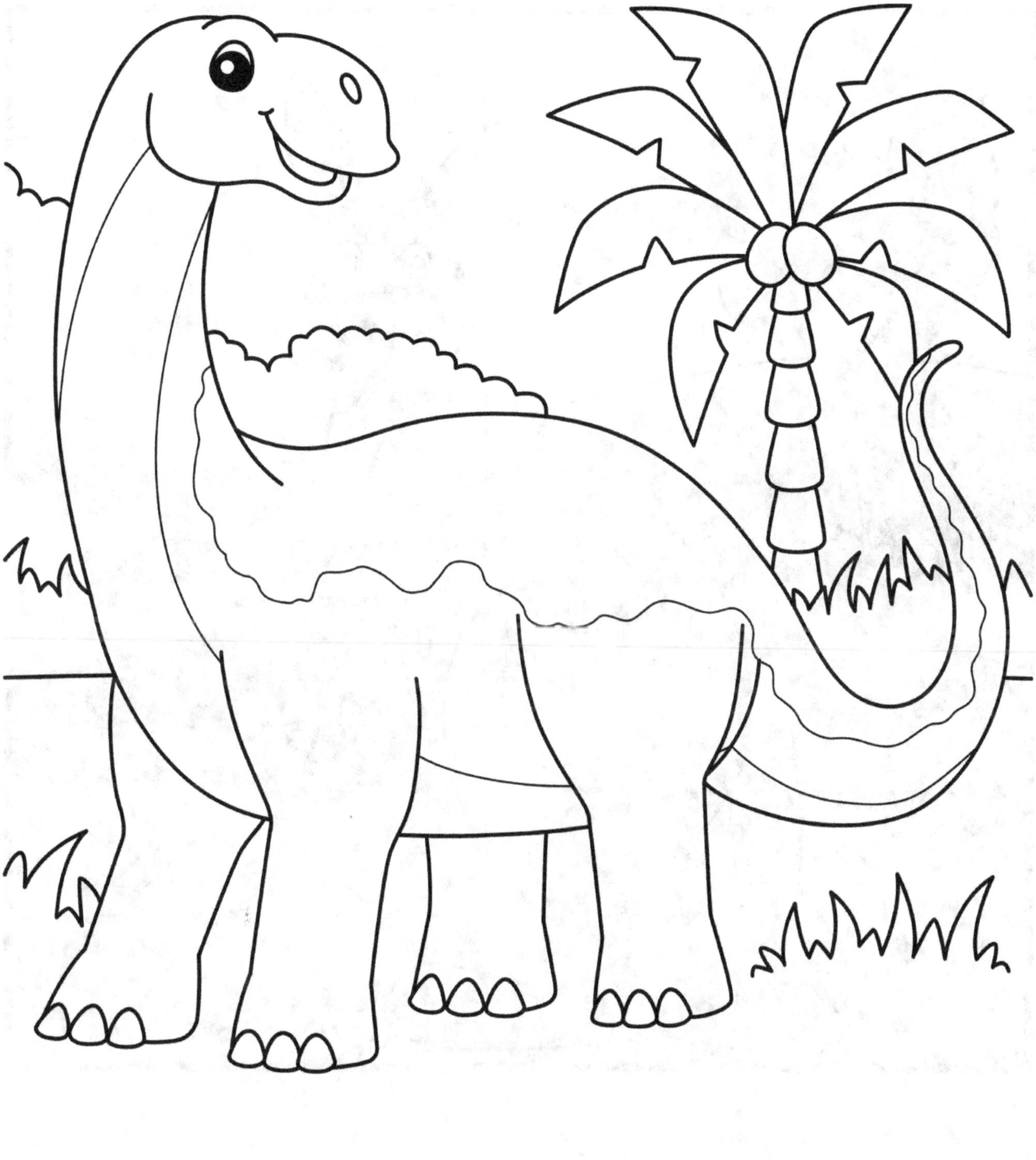

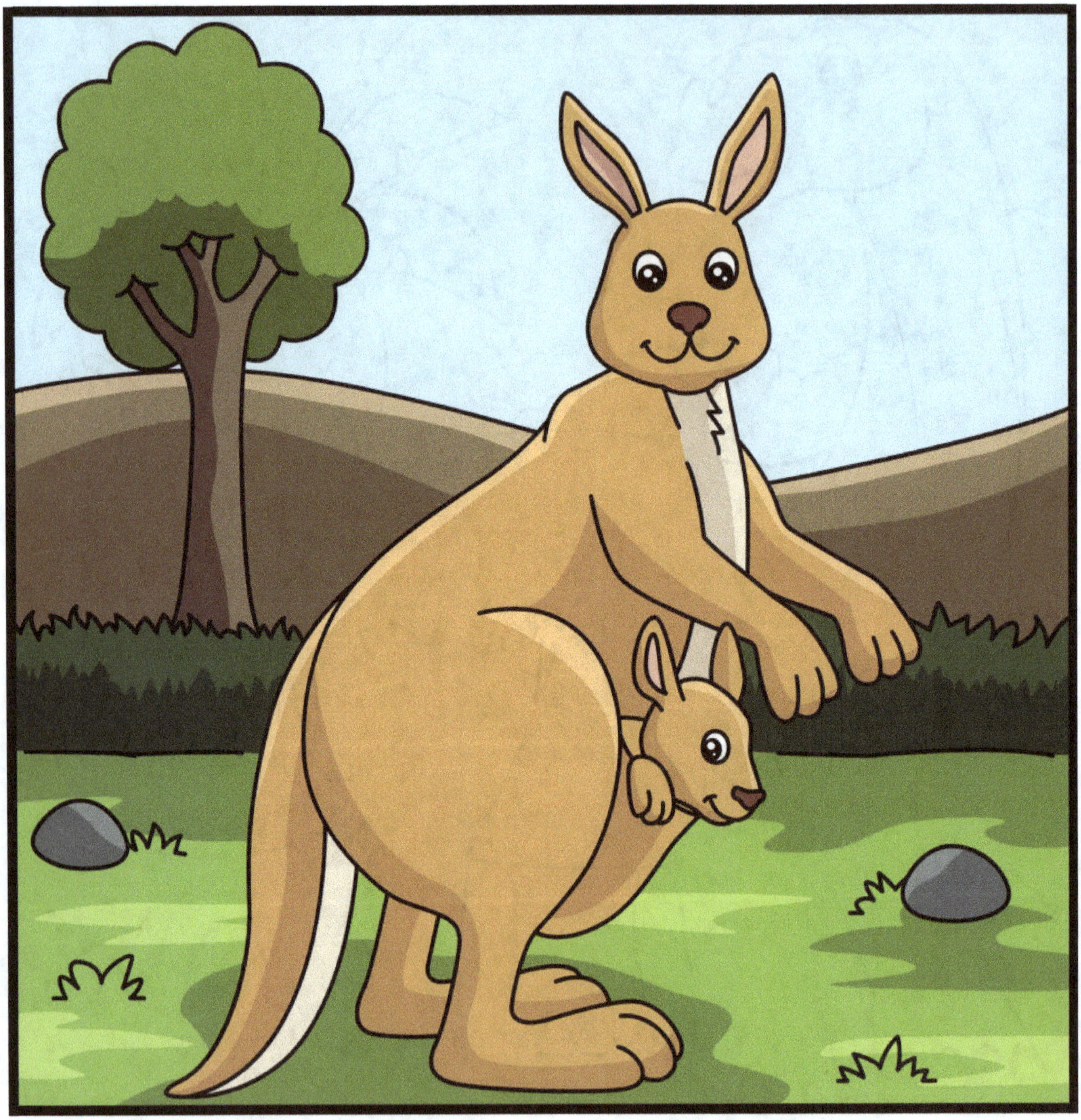

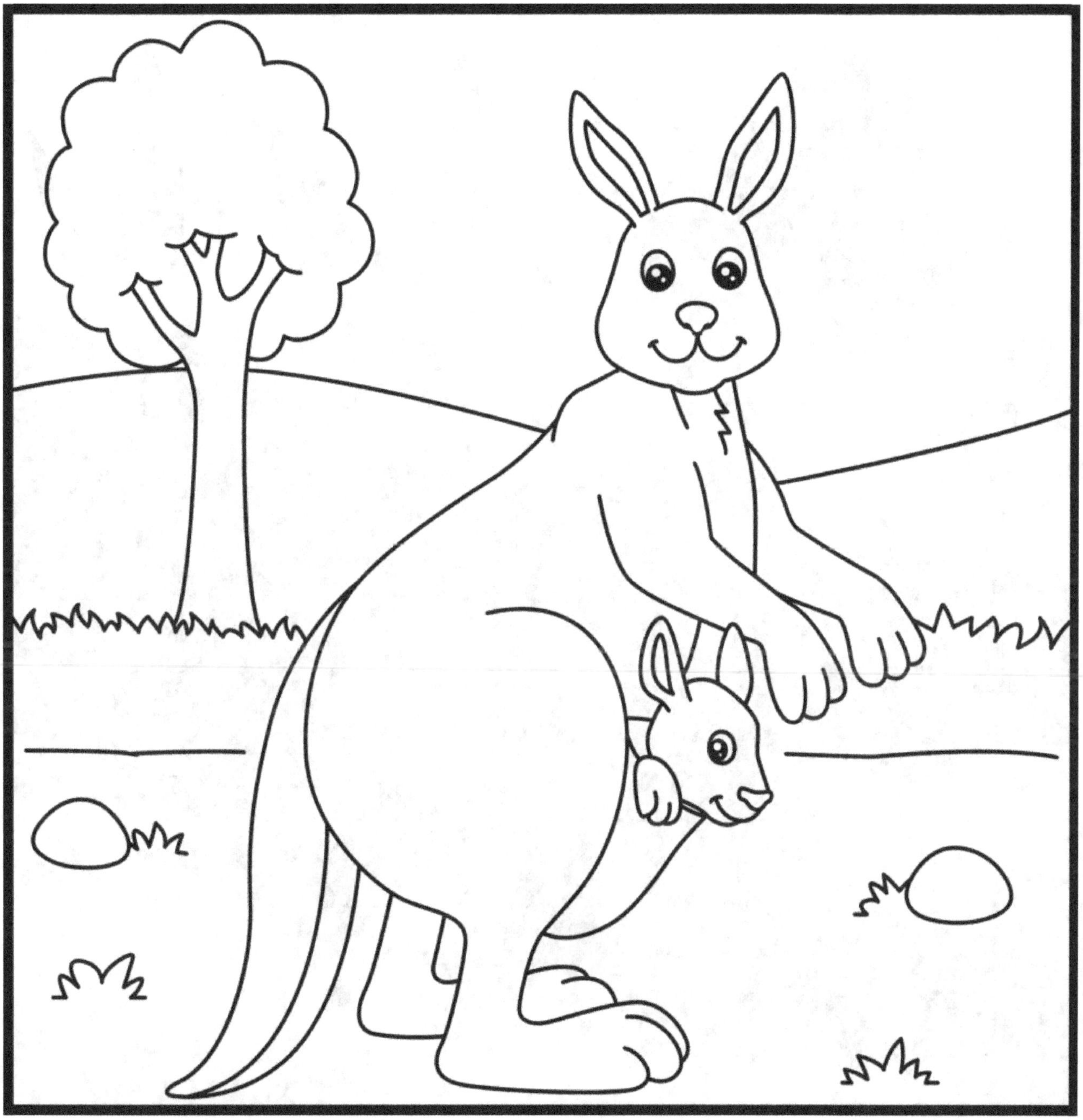

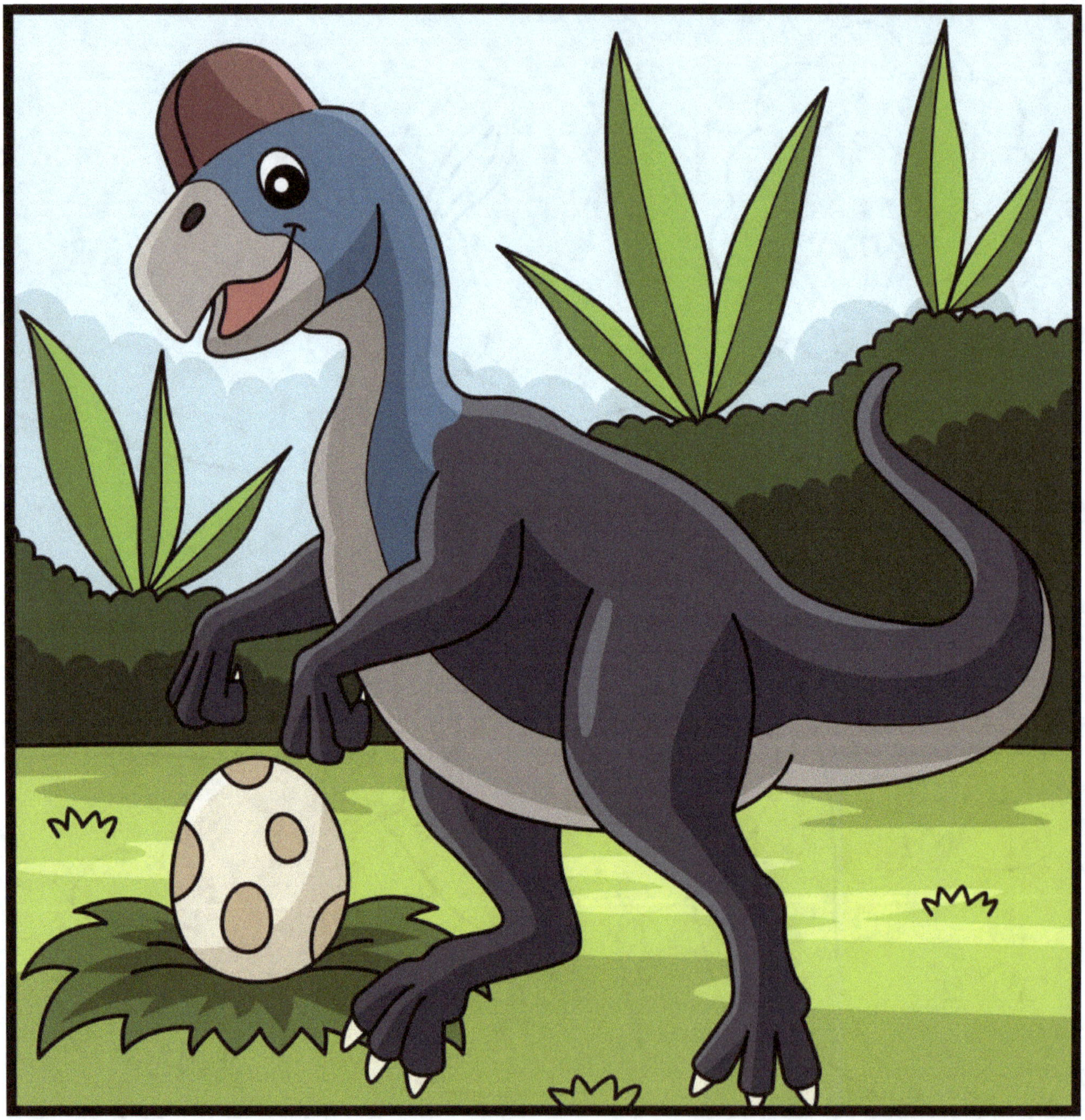

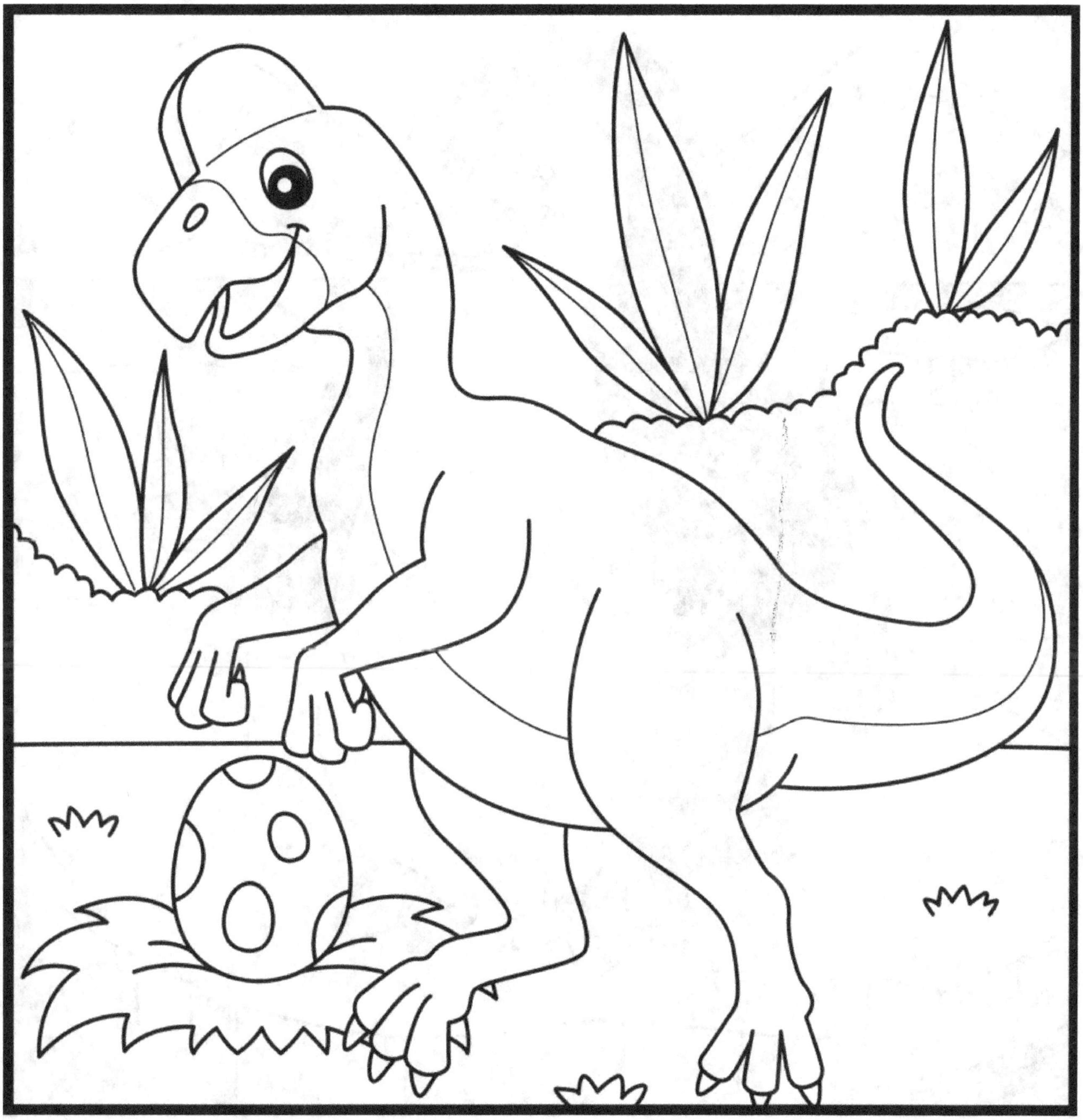

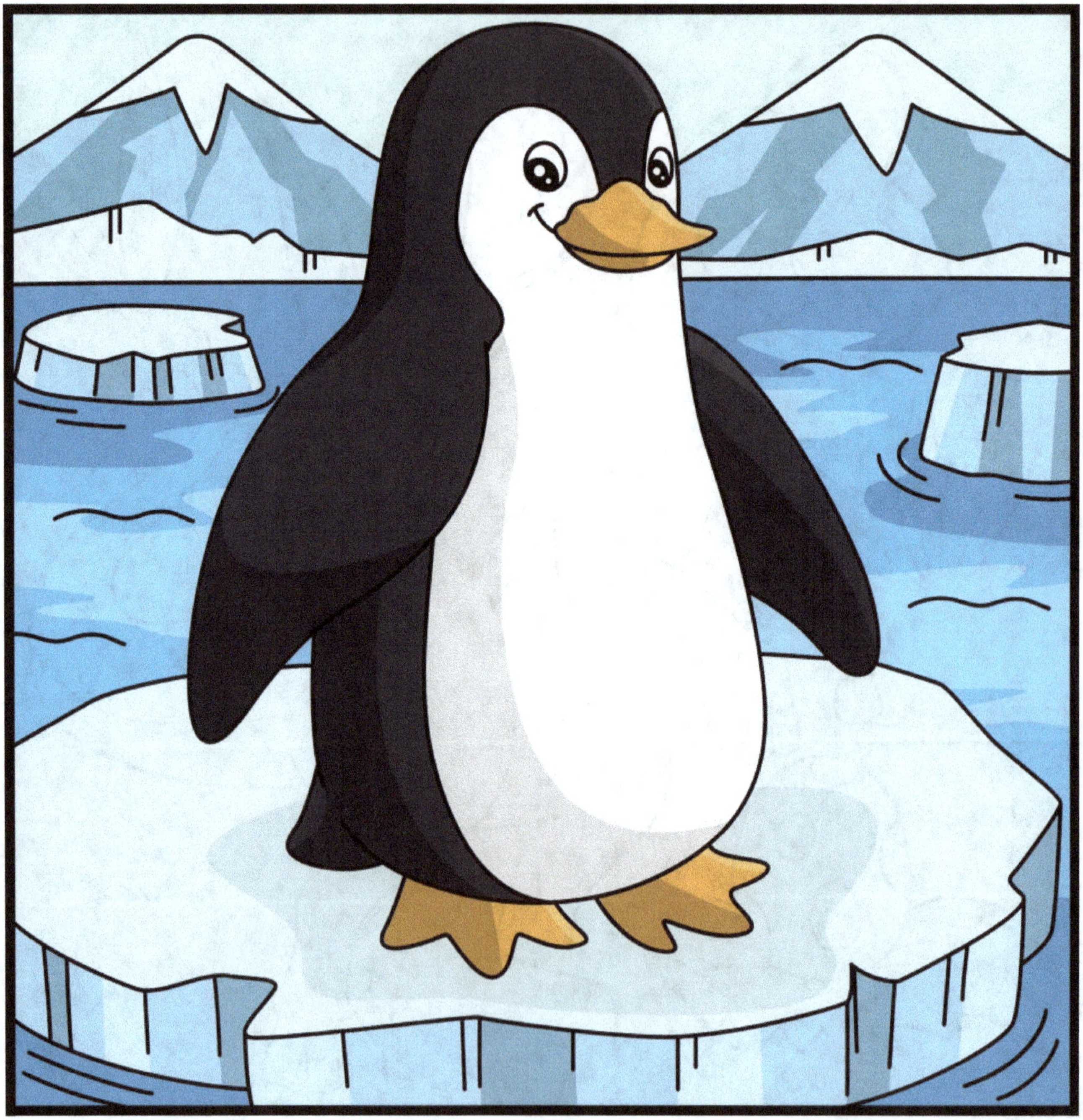

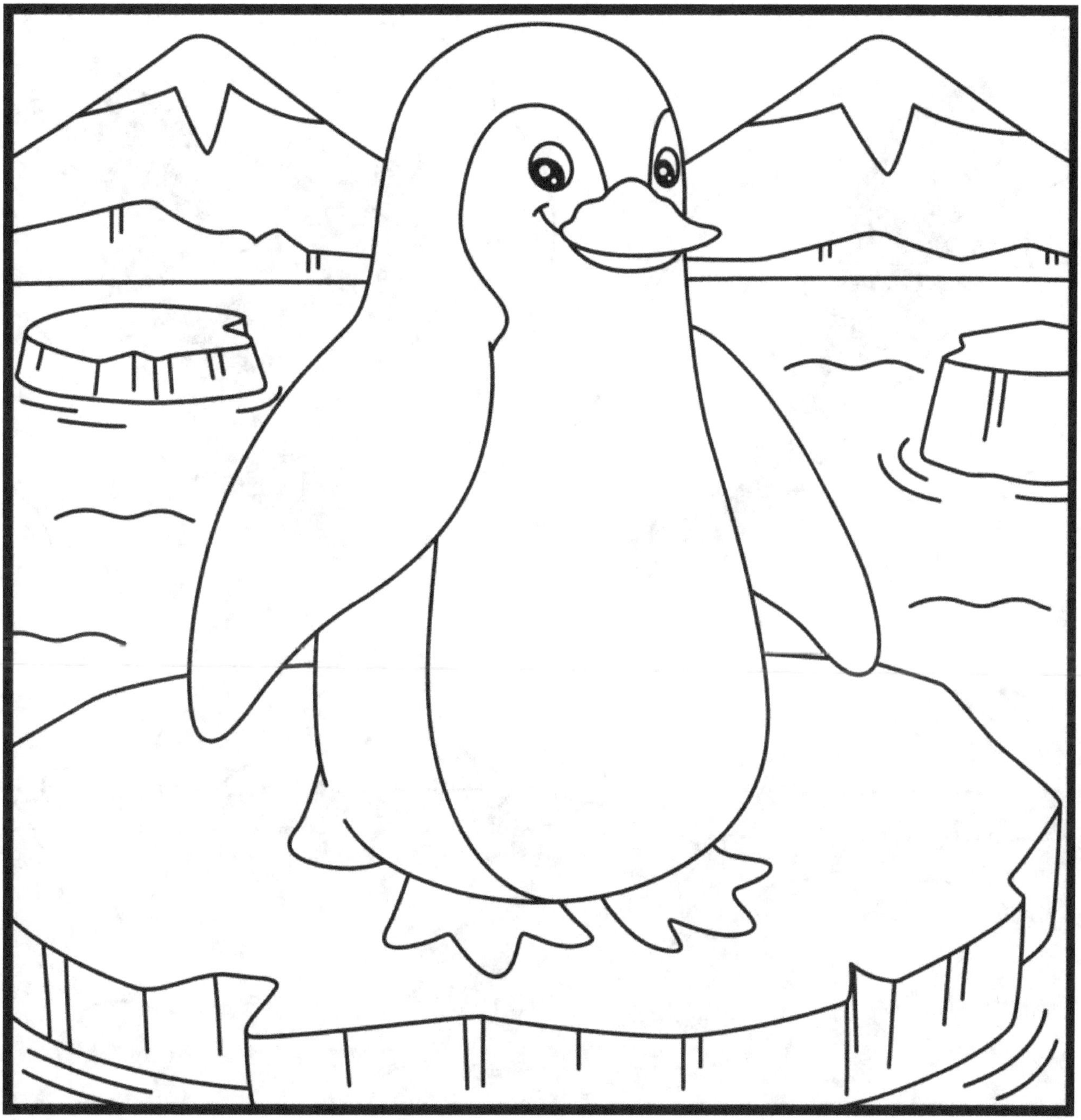

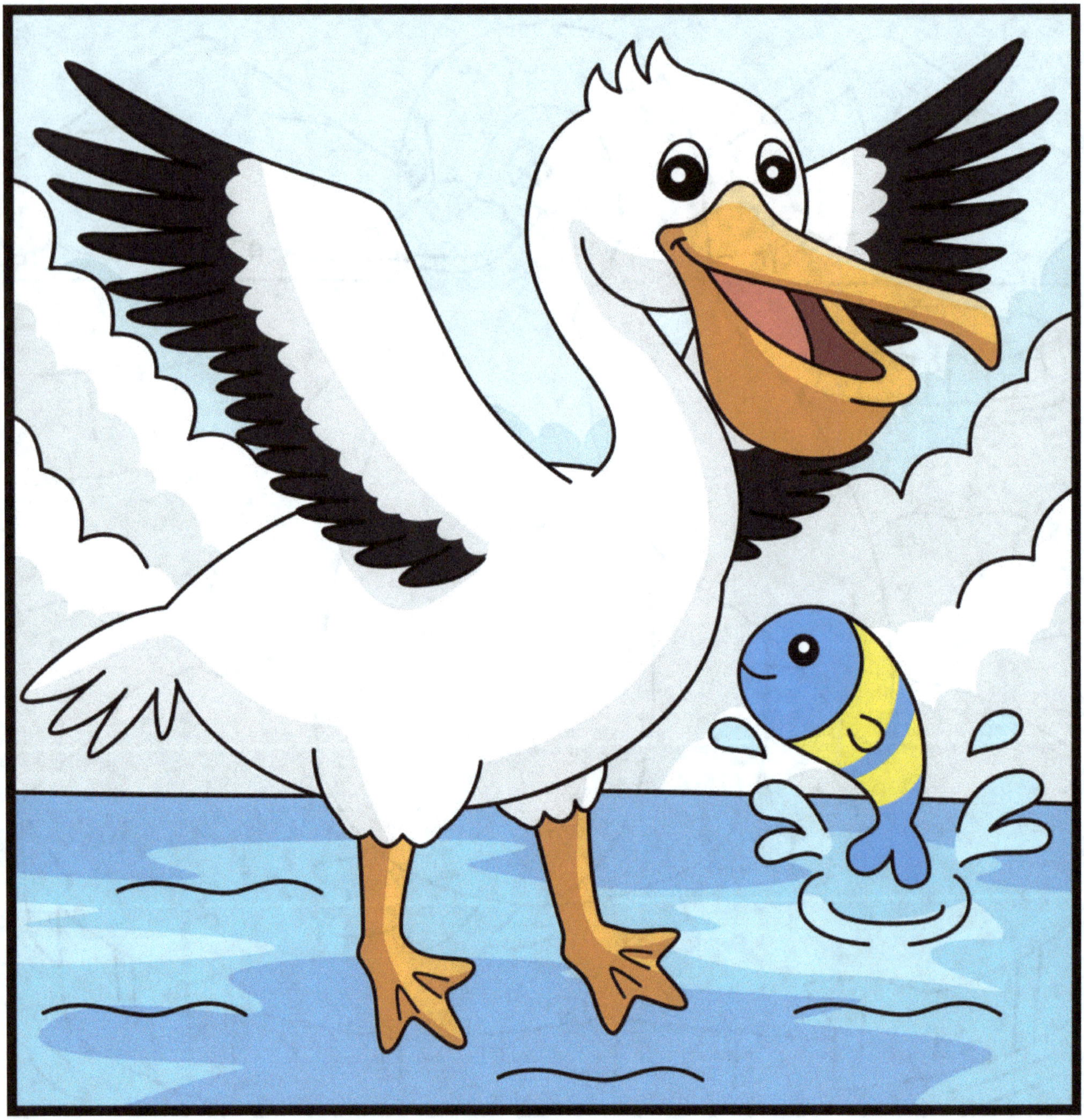

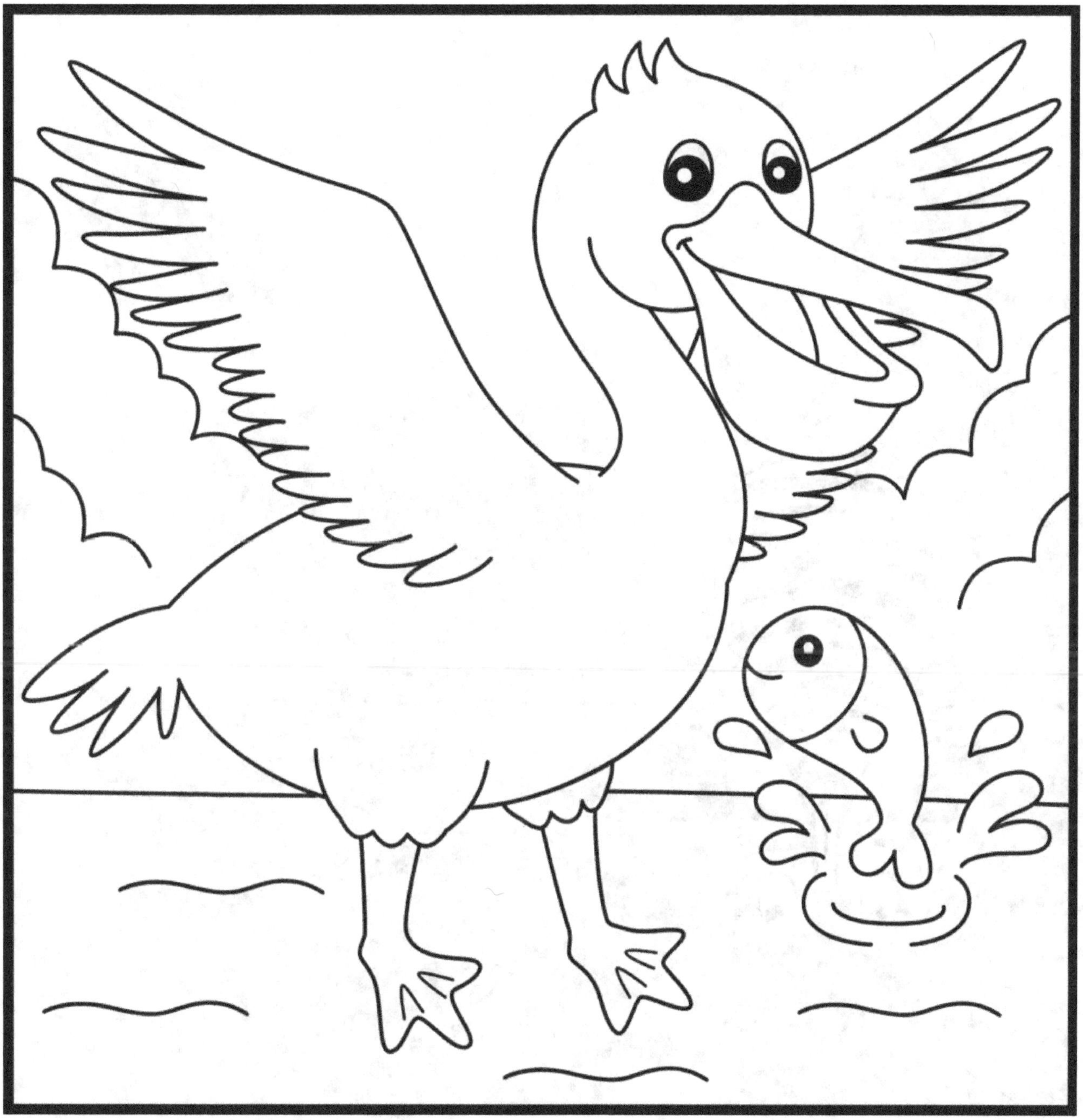

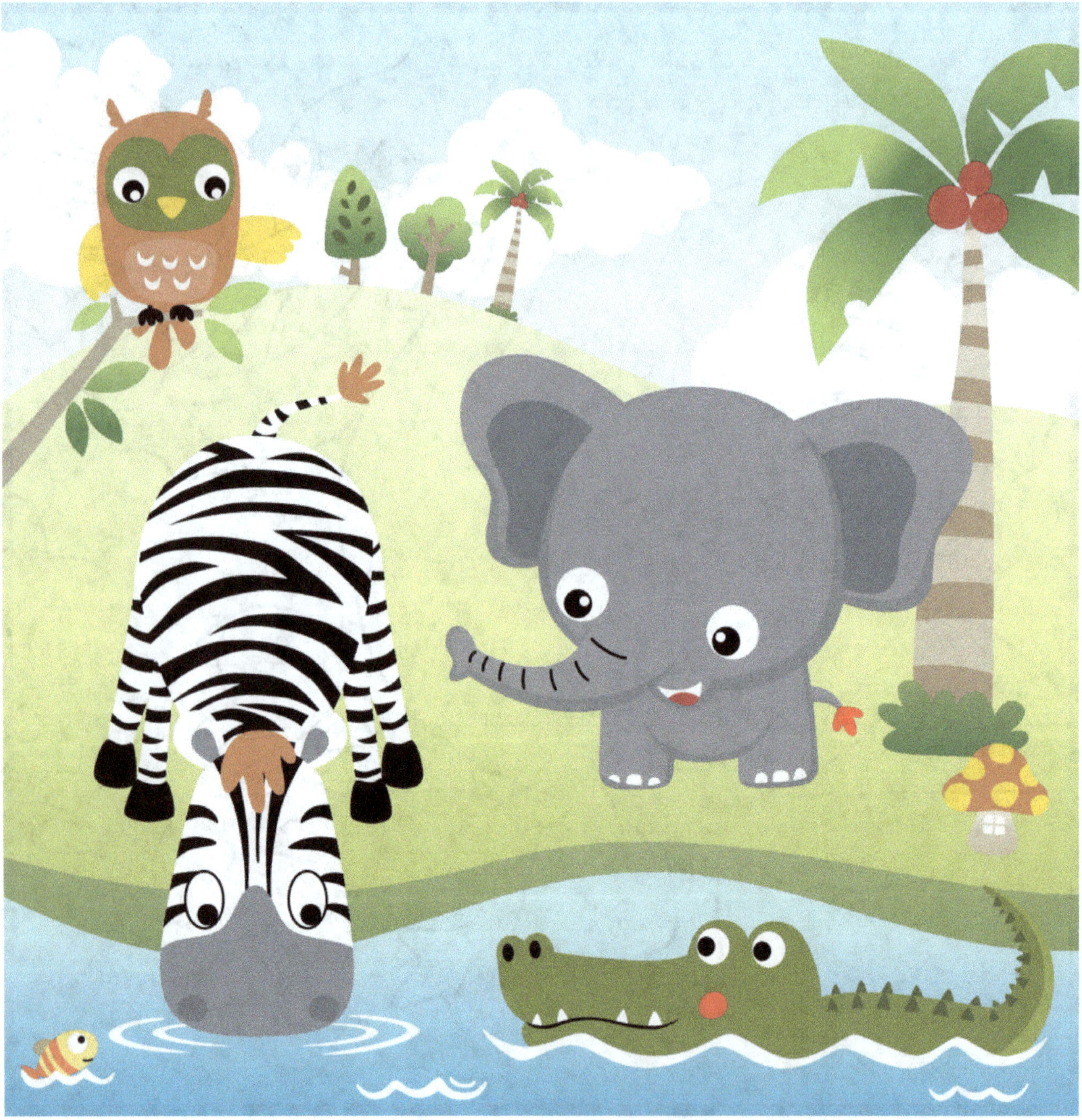

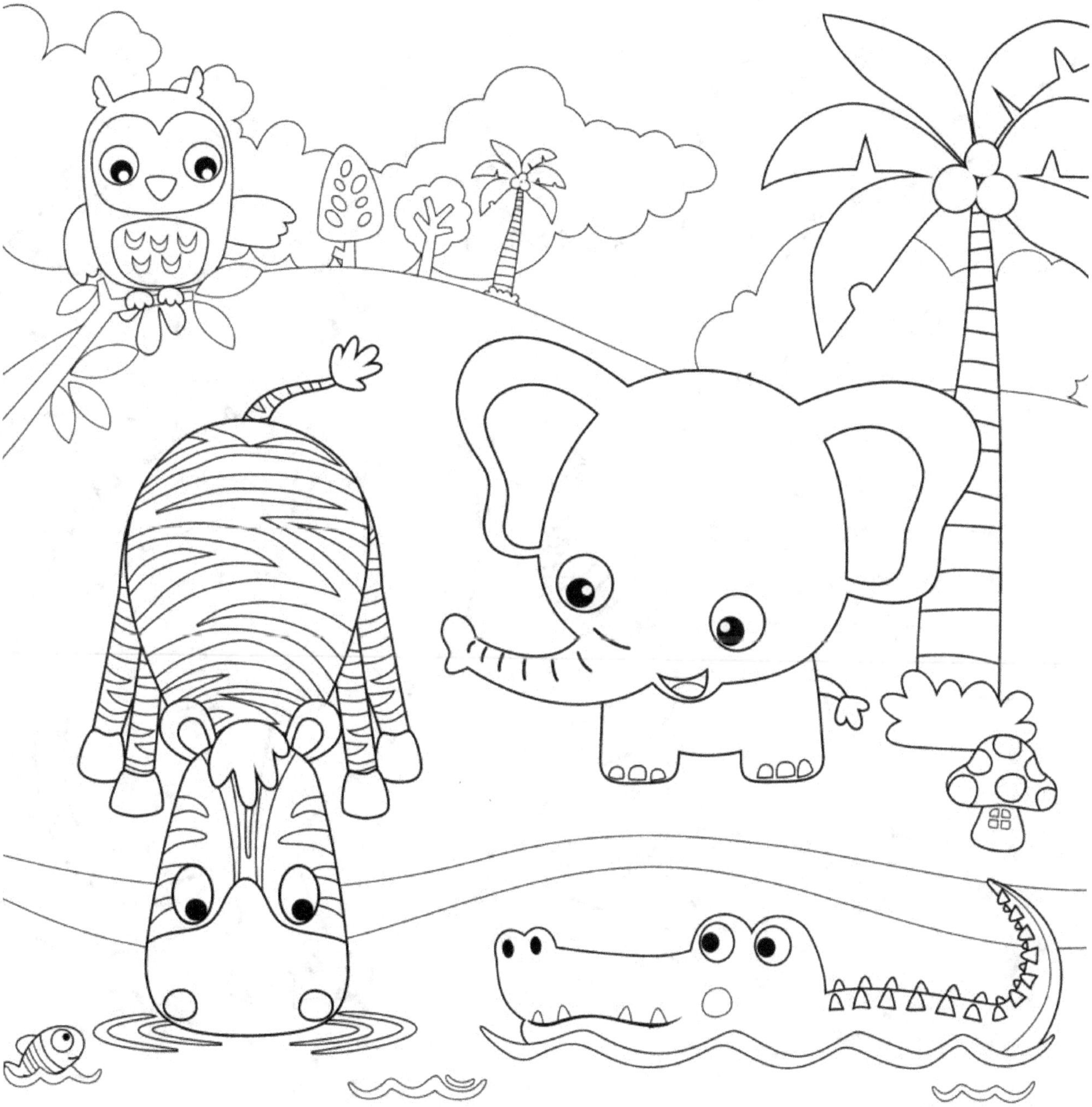

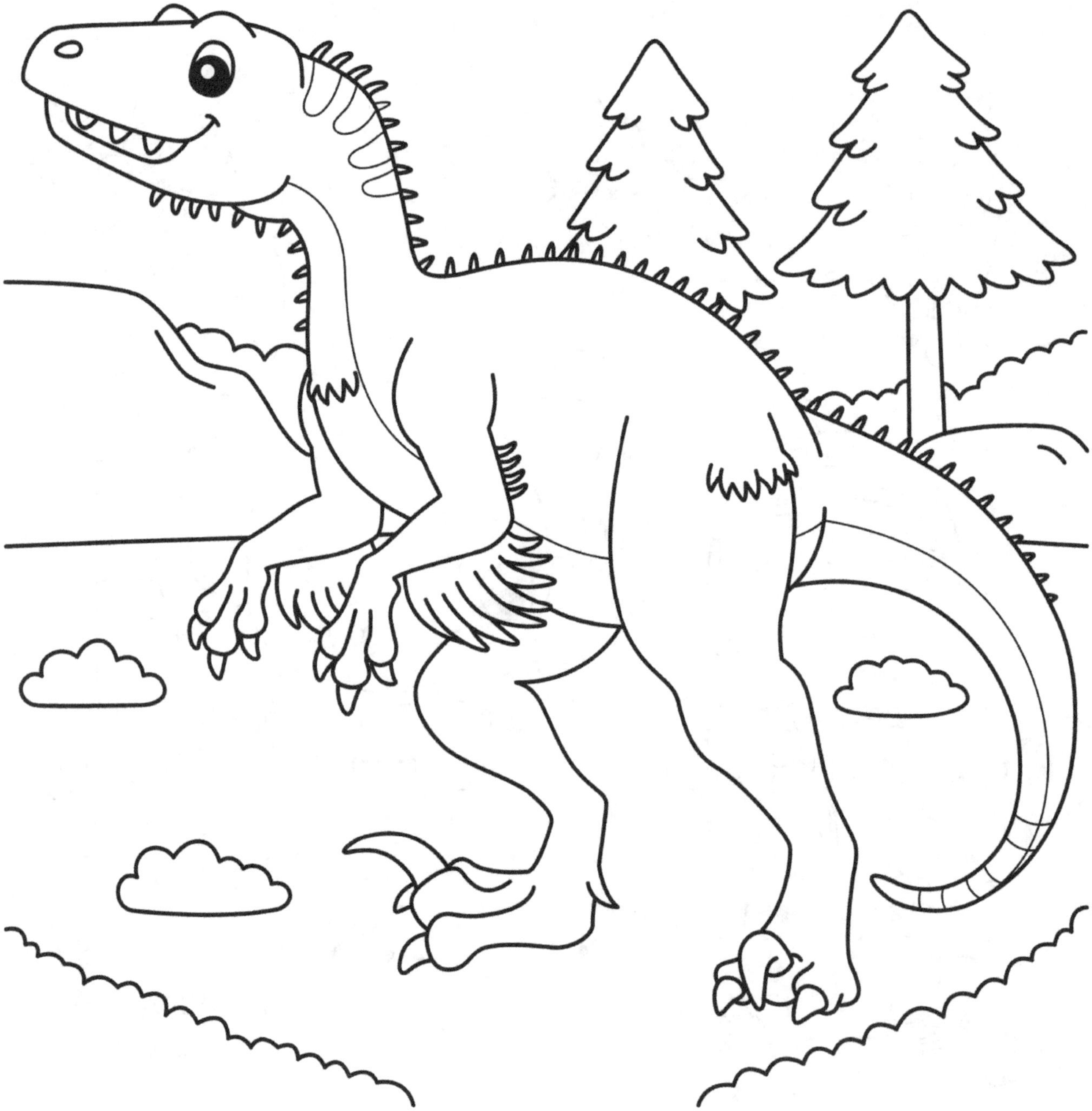

www.ingramcontent.com/pod-product-compliance
Lightning Source LLC
Chambersburg PA
CBHW080609220526
45466CB00010B/3300
* 9 7 9 8 3 9 3 7 5 8 4 3 1 *